Values for Educational Leadership

Values for Educational Leadership

Graham Haydon

SAGE Publications
Los Angeles • London • New Delhi • Singapore

SAGE Publications Ltd
1 Oliver's Yard
55 City Road
London EC1Y 1SP

SAGE Publications Inc
2455 Teller Road
Thousand Oaks, California 91320

SAGE Publications India Pvt Ltd
B 1/I 1 Mohan Cooperative Industrial Area
Mathura Road
New Delhi 110 044

SAGE Publications Asia-Pacific Pte Ltd
33 Pekin Street #02–01
Far East Square
Singapore 048763

Library of Congress Control Number: 2006938799

A catalogue record for this book is available from the British Library

ISBN-978-1-4129-3467-1
ISBN-978-1-4129-3468-8 (pbk)

Typeset by Pantek Arts Ltd, Maidstone, Kent
Printed in India at Replika Press Pvt. Ltd.
Printed on paper from sustainable resources

Contents

Acknowledgements

This book is based on materials prepared for a module within a distance learning course on Applied Educational Leadership and Management offered by the External Programme of the University of London. I would like to thank Marianne Coleman for her initial invitation to me to write those materials; Derek Glover for supplying two case studies that are used in this book (fictionalised studies that are based on extensive experience and research); and my colleagues Anne Gold, Megan Crawford and Janet Orchard for valuable comment and discussion on a number of the topics covered.

Introduction

Reading can be a passive experience, in a way that conversation is not. This book will lose much of its point if you passively assimilate the ideas in it. I hope you will be challenged and stimulated to think for yourselves about values in educational leadership, in the way that you would be in a direct conversation.

Let's start with your reasons for picking up this book. I shall assume that you are someone who is in a leadership role in education, or aspires to be in such a role. Of course, your interest may be less direct than that. Perhaps you are studying education in an academic course without intending to take a leadership role. If so, you will still find a lot in this book that can be relevant to your studies. But if you already have or you want to have a leadership role, then your interest will not be purely academic. You will want what you read to make some difference to what you think and what you do.

Values, after all, are not primarily an academic subject. Of course, values can be studied academically, but they are also an integral part of everyone's experience. You already know a lot about values, because you have been gaining experience of values through your whole life up to now. Values are inescapable whenever we aim at something or decide what to do or not to do.

But your lifetime's experience does not necessarily mean that you have a very *clear* understanding of values or that you can very readily articulate what your own values are, or engage in discussion with others about their values. Many people find this difficult. Most people are not very used to serious systematic reflection about their own values or the values they encounter in the world around them.

We all know we live in a world in which there seem to be many different ideas about values. This might encourage us to think hard about our own values and how far we share or don't share them with other people. But there are other features of our lives that don't encourage this kind of reflection; we are so busy that we don't have much time for reflection, we have to take a lot of things for granted, we have to get on with the job.

Now that your job involves leadership, or you hope that it will, you will be busier than ever. Even so, this is a good time to stop and *think* about values. In fact, it's not just a good idea to do that, it's essential. Leadership, though it's open to many interpretations, surely in some way involves giving a lead to others and that lead has to be in some direction. Which direction? That is already a question of values.

But isn't it the job of educational leaders these days just to aim at the targets that are set for them by government, by legislation, by state policy? Isn't effectiveness in achieving the aims everything? Well, effectiveness is one value, but it's not the only one. And it's surely not the job of leaders in education to be *unreflectively* pursuing ends laid down for them. Ends can be evaluated for how worthwhile they are. And besides, some ways of achieving the ends may be OK and other ways unacceptable – which is another question of values.

So the aim of this book is above all to encourage you to reflect on values, and to introduce you to ideas and arguments that will serve you as resources in doing that. You might still have more than one kind of reason for reading this book. Perhaps you are working for a qualification, such as the National Professional Qualification for Headteachers in England, and you will not get that qualification unless you can say something and write something sensible about the values that will influence your work as a head. So for you, thinking about values will be, at least partly, a means to an end. That is a perfectly respectable reason for thinking about values, but not the only one. You may feel – I hope you will – that even if you don't have to prove anything to anyone else, you would rather be clear than muddled in your own approach to educational leadership, rather have a firm sense of what matters to you than be confused about it. If you feel that, then we know already that you value clear thinking and self-knowledge. I hope this book will encourage you to engage in the first – which will sometimes mean questioning the ideas that your leadership role exposes you to – and that in the process it may even help you towards the second.

Where is this book coming from?

I mentioned above that values can be studied academically. This is true of values in relation to leadership as much as in any other context. Because values are unavoidable in leadership and management, much of the work in that field contains some reference to values whether or not that is explicitly the main theme. In the academic literature on educational leadership, values are treated in a variety of ways. Some writers, following well-established methods within the social sciences, report on the values that managers and leaders hold and about how these values influence what they do. This book will refer to some of that work, and to other ideas and possibilities that might be tested or established by the methods of the social sciences, but its main concern is different.

There is one academic subject in particular – outside of academia it might be better called an approach or a way of thinking – that aims to help people get clear about their ideas and their assumptions, and whether these ideas and assumptions have any good grounding or not. That subject is philosophy. In this book I hope to show you the value of approaching questions in the kind of way that philosophers do – with careful attention, for instance, to the concepts and arguments we use and whether we have good reason for thinking what we do think.

When philosophy focuses on values – on questions, for instance, about what is right and wrong, and how we can know – it is called moral philosophy or ethics. When philosophy focuses on education – on questions, for instance, about the aims of education and what counts as a good education – it is called philosophy of education. So, academically speaking, the resources that this book draws on, in addition to the wider literature on educational leadership, will be ethics and philosophy of education.

I shall not be trying to make you into a philosopher in an academic sense, but I shall certainly be asking you to think for yourself about many value-laden ideas that will make a difference to the way you approach leadership.

That does not mean that the academic literature on educational leadership is neglected. Any serious study of the field will need to take into account a variety of work by a variety of writers. This book will refer to many works by well-known writers on educational leadership, helping you to locate the ideas in this book within that larger literature.

The structure of this book

It will help you to work through this book if you understand at the beginning why it is constructed as it is. The whole field of interest that we might label as 'values in educational leadership' is vast and rather amorphous. Some way is needed of dividing it up. Different ways are possible, but the one chosen here is as follows.

First, we need as much clarity as we can get about the nature of values. This is the main task of Chapter 1. Because, as I said above, you already have a lot of experience of values, even if you have not thought about them systematically, this chapter starts by asking you to think about your response to some of the questions that are commonly raised about values. Where do our values come from? What sort of grounding can be given to values? Are all values really subjective? Are they relative to cultures?

The same chapter is also the first opportunity for sorting out the different ways in which values can make a difference to the work of educational leaders. Values can function as goals, but they can also put constraints on how we pursue our goals. And besides the states of affairs that we may aim to bring about, we can value certain qualities that we may look for both in individuals and in organisations. Distinctions along these lines provide the framework for the following chapters.

Chapter 2 looks at the purposes of education. We see that various parties may have different ideas about what the aims or purposes of education should be. Leaders in education need to be able to think about these various possible purposes. On what basis are competing purposes for education to be judged? What are the implications of saying, in a phrase that is becoming popular in the language of leadership, that leaders in education must have a *moral purpose*?

Chapter 3 concentrates on the individual leader. First we look at the kind of authority that may be involved in being a leader. Then we ask about the qualities that are desirable in a leader, identifying qualities of two kinds: the motivation to follow important principles, and desirable personal qualities of the kind that can be called *virtues*.

Chapter 4 takes up the idea of *vision* that has become popular in recent discourse about leadership. We try to see what is meant by 'vision' in this context and tackle several difficulties in the idea. This chapter concludes with one particular example of what a vision for education can look like.

Chapter 5 looks at values in the context of culture: both a school's culture and the surrounding culture. We look at several case studies in which a school's culture is affected in different ways by the school's leadership and by the surrounding culture, and we ask how far a leader can deliberately change a school's culture.

Chapter 6 looks at the desirability of a school being a community, where a community is characterised in terms of the sharing of values. We explore the connections between community and democracy and ask how far democratic leadership is possible in education.

Occasionally in all of these chapters a passage in italics will ask you a direct question or set you a reflective task. You should be prepared to stop and think at these points before continuing with the text. Writing down your response will help you to organise your thoughts. If this book is being used as a text in a course it will be easy to adapt these activities as opportunities for group discussion.

1 | Values and their place in educational leadership

If you approach your thinking about values by way of your experience of leadership or your reading about it, you may bring various preconceptions with you. There is already a mass of ideas available in the academic literature and the professional literature about what leaders should do and how they should think. This chapter, after a brief opening section, will reverse the order: it will ask you to think about values in general, before thinking about educational leadership or even about education. Later in the chapter we will bring the discussion back to education by looking directly at a number of ways in which values can make a difference to educational thinking.

This chapter will help you to:

- understand why values are vital in educational leadership;
- articulate what you take values to be, and which values are important to you;
- be aware of a variety of answers to the question 'where do values come from?';
- reflect on the difference between moral or ethical values, and other values;
- be aware of a variety of ways in which values can impinge on educational decision-making.

After a brief introduction reviewing why values are important in educational leadership, this chapter has four main sections: what are values? where do our values come from? morality and ethics; how do values make a difference in education?

Why are values important in educational leadership?

It is not difficult to find answers to this question within the academic literature on leadership and management, but many answers give only part of the picture. For instance, the following statement by Willower has been quoted by a number of writers:

Because a significant portion of the practice in educational administration requires rejecting some courses of action in favour of a preferred one, values are generally acknowledged to be central to the field. (Willower, 1992, quoted in Begley and Leonard, 1999: 51. Willower is using the term 'administration' in the American sense which, in educational contexts, approximately equates to 'leadership')

Willower's statement is not false, but it does illustrate the sort of preconception to which I have already referred: in this case, the idea that values are important because they come into *decisions*. Certainly the decisions we make turn on values, but is that the only way in which values come into our lives – either our professional or our personal lives? There is more to educational leadership than making a decision from time to time, and it would be surprising if values only made a difference when there is a decision between alternatives to be made (as if everything else in educational leadership is somehow a value-free sphere). By the end of this chapter you should be aware of a number of other ways in which values are important in educational leadership.

First, though, we need to understand more about values in general. The following sections will ask you to think about your own values, personally as well as professionally.

What are values?

In entering on a distinct area of enquiry it is natural to want some clarification about exactly what we are meant to be studying. Sometimes we find that a definition of terms is helpful. But definitions need to be treated with some caution. 'Values' is not a technical term. In talking about values, we are talking about something which is part of the experience of everyone. You already in your life have a lot of experience of values, though you may not have spent a lot of time in thinking about your values or articulating them. This chapter will encourage you to do that. So it is best to start, not by giving you a definition, but by asking you to think about what you recognise as the values that you take to be important.

Before you read any further, try to call to mind some values that you are sure are important. Then see if you can write down two lists:

- *values that you think are important for anyone;*
- *values that you take to be especially important for you, in your own life.*

(Later we shall come to values that may be especially important in educational leadership. It does not matter if some of the same items come into more than one list.)

It is often easier to list examples of some kind of thing than it is to give a definition. For instance, you would find it easy to list some examples of fruit but more difficult (unless you happen to be a botanist) to give a definition of fruit. The same applies to values, though even to list examples of values may be more difficult than listing examples of fruit.

I do not know, of course, what you will have listed, but I can make some guesses, and these underlie the next few paragraphs.

In the first list, it is possible that you have written down some abstract terms such as 'justice', 'truth', 'goodness', 'health', 'happiness', 'love' – of course there could be many other such terms.

In the second list, you may have repeated some items. But you may also have mentioned some things that are more personal to you. This might be doing well in your job, or having a good relationship with your family, or many other things.

Is there anything in common so far about all the things you have listed? One guess is that you have probably not included in your lists any concrete physical objects. For instance, while it may be important to you to live with your family in a comfortable house – this may be something you value – you have probably not written 'my house' in your second list.

I may be wrong about this. Some of the writers in the literature of educational leadership, when they talk about values, have included physical objects in their lists. To me, while there is no doubt that we can value particular objects – a vase which I have inherited from my grandmother might for instance have great sentimental value to me, and my computer may have great usefulness to me (another word for 'usefulness' here is 'instrumental value', and we shall come back to that idea) – it would seem odd to me to include 'my grandmother's vase' or 'my computer' in a list of my values.

You will have to see if you agree with this. We are talking for the moment – as philosophers often do – about how we use words, and words can be used rather differently by different speakers, especially by different speakers of an international language like English. To me, a value has to be something less tangible than a physical object: it might be justice, it might be my relationship with my family, it might be having a comfortable house, but it is not actually the house itself.

In a moment I shall ask you to think whether you can suggest a definition of values. Before that, there are two more points worth thinking about. One is about importance. I asked you to list values that you take to be important. That leaves open the possibility that there may be unimportant values. In their book on *The Ethics of School Administration*, the authors Strike, Haller and Soltis (1998: 36–7) give as an example of a value statement:

'Pickles are better than olives.'

This example has nothing to do with school leadership, of course, and there is nothing wrong with that. If we are trying to get as clear as we can about our *concept* of values, it is best not to get involved at the same time in contentious questions on which people might have serious disagreements. That can come later. It often helps our understanding if we start with easy examples and then move on to more difficult ones. The problem in this case is that I am not sure whether most people would count 'pickles are better than olives' as a value statement at all. It is certainly, as the authors say, an expression of a personal preference. We shall have to say more later about the relationship between values and preferences. For the moment, you could say either of two things: *either* this expression of a preference is so clearly just that – an expression of a preference and nothing more – that we would not seriously count it as a value statement at all; *or* it is an example of a value statement, but the value in question is a thoroughly trivial one. It does not matter which of these things you are inclined to say, provided you recognise that if we can count this claim 'pickles are better than olives' as a value statement at all, it is a trivial case. Outside of academic examples, we are more likely to talk about values – actually using that word – when we think there is something of importance at stake.

The second point for the moment is that values can affect what people do. Even in the trivial case just mentioned, if someone thinks pickles are better than olives, she is likely to choose pickles when offered a choice between the two. In more important cases, if you value harmonious relationships within your family more than success in your job, or the other way round, this is likely to make a difference if you have to choose, say, whether to apply for a promotion which will take you further away from your home.

Keeping in mind the points about values made so far, see if you can suggest a definition of values.

Here is a definition, attributable in its original version to the sociologist Kluckhohn, which has been cited by several writers on values in educational management:

> Values are conceptions, explicit or implicit, distinctive of an individual or characteristic of a group, of the desirable which influence the selection from available modes, means and ends of action. (Quoted with minor changes from Begley, 2003: 3)

Compare this with the definition you have thought of. Does Kluckhohn's definition seem to fit your own understanding of values? If not, what would you want to change in the definition?

Here are some comments on Kluckhohn's definition, following the order of the points mentioned in it:

- That values are conceptions seems to fit the examples we have mentioned so far. We have suggested that values are not physical objects but ideas about what is important or what matters to us.
- Values may be explicit or implicit. If you say that one of your values is justice or truth then you are making this value explicit. But in your choices and actions you will be influenced all the time by what you take to be preferable or important, whether or not you spell out to yourself or to anyone else exactly what ideas are influencing you.
- Values may be distinctive of an individual: perhaps some personal experience has given you an aspiration for your own life which other people do not share. But values can also be distinctive of a group. A religious community, for instance, may hold certain values which are different from those of other groups. (It is important here that values, like ideas generally, do not exist just in the heads of individuals. Ideas are recorded in writing and in symbolism of many kinds – in religious ritual, for instance.)
- Values are conceptions of what is desirable. 'Desirable' means something like 'worthy to be desired', and this may be different from what actually is desired. If you are a smoker, but you think you ought to give it up, then you will often desire a cigarette but what you think is desirable is that you stop smoking and cease to have a craving for cigarettes. Then being free of such a habit is one of your values – one of your conceptions of what is desirable.
- Kluckhohn says that values 'influence the selection from available modes, means and ends of action'. This makes the important point that there is a link between values and motivation. Whenever we are doing something deliberately – and not only when we are consciously deciding to take one course of action and reject another, as the statement from Willower might suggest – our values will be influencing us in what we do and how we do it, even though we may not have spelled out our reasons for acting in one way rather than another.

At this point there is another question for you to think about. Do our values always *influence us?*

You are probably familiar with the idea of paying *lip service* to values. This means that someone says that something is important but does not act accordingly. For instance, a male headteacher may say that gender equality is important, but actually take no action to prevent practices that discriminate against girls and women. Does he, then, recognise the importance of gender equality at all?

Possibly he does, in a sense. Perhaps we should not be too ready to say, without further details about the case, that such a teacher neglects the value of equality altogether. The idea that there is a connection between values and actions is correct, but it is not a straightforward connection.

Where do our values come from?

This is a question often asked about values. It is one way of expressing a set of concerns about values that often worry people. Can we be confident that the values we are following are the right ones?

If we *are* confident, then how should we respond towards people who appear to hold different values from our own?

If we are *not* confident, then can we find some sort of firm grounding for the values we are following? If not, then is it alright just to follow our own values in our own way? In private life this might be possible. But for anyone working in education there are further questions. Many decisions are made which make a difference to the lives of young people as they grow up. Are teachers perhaps just imposing the values they happen to hold onto these young people? And are educational leaders imposing *their* values onto teachers?

Because such questions can always be raised, we need to look further into where values come from and what sort of justification they can be given.

On this issue, in the context of educational leadership and administration, the work of Christopher Hodgkinson has been influential for several decades. He has offered a framework for thinking about the sources of people's values that has been adopted for different purposes by various writers (e.g. by Begley (2003) in an article already cited) and criticised by others (see Richmon (2003 and 2004) for an appreciative but critical stance).

It is useful to have some acquaintance with Hodgkinson's ideas because other writers in the field so often refer to him. And his framework is useful for addressing the question we have asked here, about where values come from and how they can be justified. The most important point to grasp here is that there is no single answer to this question: instead there are several kinds of answer, each of which will seem to fit different cases. On this point Hodgkinson and his critics would agree, even though they would offer some different ways of dividing up the whole field of values.

Hodgkinson introduced and discussed his framework in several places (e.g. Hodgkinson, 1991: ch. 5) with some variation in the details. He categorises several sources of values. At one end of the framework are values based simply in preferences. We do not usually expect people to give reasons for their simple preferences (for example, I would not ask you for your reason for preferring your coffee black). Hodgkinson calls values that are simply a matter of preference 'subrational'.

Next there are values that Hodgkinson thinks can be given a rational justification, by appealing either to consensus or to consequences. Then at the other end of the framework there are values that are matters of principle, expressing commitments that (in Hodgkinson's view) go beyond the possibility of rational grounding. Hodgkinson calls these values 'transrational'. They might include principles of justice, equality or dignity.

In ordinary English we may think of the principles that Hodgkinson calls 'transrational' either as fundamental principles that underpin all our other values, or as high-level principles that are somehow placed above all our other values. Both of these ways of thinking involve a spatial metaphor. So if we represent Hodgkinson's framework in a diagram, we can put the transrational values either at the bottom or at the top (you may find diagrams of both sorts in the leadership literature). Here, because it is convenient to say more about preferences first, we can use the following table as a reminder of the framework:

Hodgkinson's categories of values:	
1.	No rational basis (subrational): values based in preferences
2.	Rational basis: values based in
	(i) consensus
	(ii) consequences
3.	No rational basis (transrational): fundamental principles

Preferences

First, then, some values may have no basis other than personal preference. I have already mentioned the example from Strike, Heller and Soltis of a 'value statement' which is simply an expression of a preference: 'Pickles are better than olives.' I questioned whether we would really, outside academic discussion, be likely to see this as a *value* statement at all. Nevertheless, in order to see how statements that we do think are about important values are different from this one, we need to be explicit about several points:

- that people do have preferences;
- that these preferences do influence people's choices and actions;
- that at least some preferences really do rest in nothing but individual taste.

The last point means that if one person says 'pickles are better than olives' and another says 'olives are better than pickles' there is no point in their arguing. There is no evidence or reasoning that one could appeal to show that the other is wrong. It really is just a matter of preference.

Some people, including some philosophers, have thought that all values are like this, in that they have no basis other than personal preference. In philosophy, slightly different versions of such views are known by the terms 'emotivism' and 'subjectivism', which you may come across in your reading. (For an argument that certain approaches to school leadership are flawed because they rest in emotivism, see Smith (2002).)

Most people think that there are many questions of values that cannot be reduced to personal preference. Suppose you came across someone who said he enjoyed smacking children, especially small children, and that he would take every opportunity he could find to do this.

That is his preference. But if you want to get him to stop doing this, you surely want to do more than tell him that your own preference is for him not to smack small children. You will think that he is doing something wrong, that he is offending against values that in some way are not just matters of personal preference.

Morality and ethics

It is at this point that we are beginning to talk about matters of right and wrong, about values that people *ought* to follow regardless of their actual preferences. So far in this section I have not said much about morals or ethics, because it is better not to assume in advance that the fields covered by 'values', 'ethics' and 'morals' or 'morality' are all the same. On this point there is no consistent practice across the literature on educational leadership. Some writers may use the term 'values' very frequently and the terms 'ethics' and 'morality' quite rarely. As Begley points out:

> In the school leadership literature, there is a pronounced tendency to adopt the word *ethics* or *moral* as an umbrella term for anything values-related ... In contrast, other scholars ... reserve the term *ethic* or principles for a particular and very special category of transrational values and employ the word *values* as a generic umbrella term for all forms of 'conceptions of the desirable'. (Begley, 2003: 4).

In this book, the usage I shall follow will be closer to the second of these patterns. This is because it does make sense to speak of values that are not moral or ethical. If you are decorating the walls of your school with pictures, you may be following certain aesthetic values in deciding which pictures to choose. This might seem to be just an exercise of personal preference, but it is not necessarily so. Art critics and teachers of art may find a lot to say about why one picture is better than another; they can give reasons for their judgements. But we would not say that their judgements are moral or ethical ones.

Look back at the lists of values you made above. Can you divide these into two categories: those that have something to do with ethics or morals and those that do not? (You may think that all the values you listed come under the same category.)

What is the difference between the two categories? What is it about one value that makes it a moral or ethical matter while another is not?

There are various ways in which people may try to separate what is a moral or ethical matter from what is not. For some purposes it may be useful to draw a distinction between 'moral' and 'ethical'. The term 'ethics' has some specialised uses. It is used to refer to professional codes or responsibilities, in the phrase 'professional ethics', though there is perhaps no good reason why the standard phrase could not be 'professional morality'. 'Ethics' is also the name of the branch of philosophy that deals with matters of morality; in this sense 'ethics' is equivalent to 'moral philosophy'. For the purposes of this book we do not need to draw a systematic distinction between morality and ethics, and I shall keep to 'morality' or 'moral values' in the following discussion.

In distinguishing moral from non-moral matters, here are some considerations that may have occurred to you:

• Moral matters seem to be about how people are treated – how people behave towards each other. So judgements about one picture being better than another are not moral judgements.
• While moral values, like other values, are conceptions of the desirable, they often seem to be more than just that. We may want to say, for instance, that being kind rather than cruel is not just desirable – it is obligatory. We have the idea that morality is binding on people in ways that other conceptions of the desirable are not.

Morality, then, cannot ultimately be a matter of personal preference (despite what some people may say about it). If there is something that it would be right for me to do (even in the face of my preferences or inclination), or something that it would be wrong for me to do (though it might suit my convenience) then by and large the same things will be right or wrong for other people too (of course, personal circumstances may make a difference, but not all the difference).

Since morality is not a matter of personal preference, it is possible to argue about what is right or wrong. We expect to be able to give some sort of reasons to back up opinions about right and wrong. But at the same time, as the example of aesthetic values shows, not just any kind of reason will make something a moral matter.

What kinds of reason, then, are relevant to *moral* judgements? At this point we can go back to Hodgkinson's framework.

Consensus

We have said that values are conceptions or ideas. While you can be enter-
taining a particular idea consciously at a particular time, it is clear too that
ideas can exist independently of any individual's thinking. Conceptions or
ideas about things are built into language and culture. Values, as conceptions of what is desirable, can be shared among people. When a particular
conception of what is valuable is shared quite widely within some group
of people, we can say there is a consensus on it.

Consensus is one of the bases that Hodgkinson gives for values.
Sometimes we see consensus as sufficient backing for a value. If a community collectively considers that something is to be done in a certain way,
often, at least within that community itself, that will be sufficient reason
for doing it this way. Norms get established within a community, and the
community comes to expect conformity to its norms.

While consensus is important, we can also see that an actual consensus
within a particular community does not have to be accepted as the final
answer on the question of where norms come from and how they can be
justified. This is clear partly because there may be a different consensus in
different communities. For instance in some places it may be accepted or
even expected that a person in a position of authority making a professional appointment will give some preference to his or her own associates or
family members; in other places this will be called *nepotism* and frowned
on as violating norms of professionalism and equity.

People sometimes suggest that ethics is relative to cultures. What is certainly true is that different cultures are different from each other in *some*
of their values and norms (that is part of what makes them different cultures). If consensus were the last word on whether particular norms should
be followed, then we could accept that all norms are relative. But in fact
we can see that consensus does not have to be the last word, because a particular consensus can be criticised. If, for instance, there is a consensus
within a particular community that women's place is in the home, then it
is still possible for that consensus to be criticised by appealing to some
other considerations.

What other considerations might these be?

Consequences

One sort of consideration is an appeal to consequences. In this particular
case we might argue that a condition of society in which women's talents
are not fully used does not in the long run bring the best consequences for
everyone concerned.

People sometimes think that appealing to consequences is not giving a
moral argument. But when you are thinking about what you ought to do

in some situation, wouldn't you usually give some attention to what the consequences will be of one course of action or another? If you are thinking morally about what you ought to do, of course you should not be concerned *only* about the consequences *for yourself*, but you certainly should be concerned about the consequences for other people who will be affected by your action. We often consider that someone has acted *irresponsibly* if they have not taken the consequences for others into account.

The point about consequences is important in education, and not least in educational leadership, because education always has to have an eye to the consequences for students of one way of teaching rather than another, one syllabus rather than another and so on, and educational leaders have to look to the consequences of their decisions for all the people they are trying to lead.

Some philosophical theories about ethics have argued that all ethics is ultimately about consequences; the best known of these theories is *utilitarianism*, which says, roughly, that all morality eventually comes down to consequences for people's happiness (John Stuart Mill's book *Utilitarianism*, written in the mid-nineteenth century, is still a good and readily available introduction). But even if we do not go that far, we can recognise that thinking about consequences must at least be a part of ethical thinking.

Fundamental principles

What else may be involved in ethical thinking? Here we come to Hodgkinson's third category, values that he calls transrational. What Hodgkinson seems to have in mind are broad principles such as appeals to justice, equality or dignity, which we may take as underlying more specific ethical norms and which we can appeal to when we are justifying more specific judgements. For instance, if we were criticising a community that believed in women's place being in the home – whatever the arguments from consensus or consequences might suggest – we might appeal to equality or to human rights.

Hodgkinson is surely right in recognising that that there are ethical principles that outweigh – or should outweigh – other sorts of consideration when we are deciding what to do. If we were going deeper into moral philosophy here, we might want to ask what it means to say that these principles exist. For our purposes here, it is enough to say that these principles do exist in the human world in which we live, they are recognised in many human cultures and we can actually make use of these ideas in conversation and argument. Suppose some policy that you are proposing to pursue is in line with your own preferences, it has in its support a consensus across your professional community and it looks as if it will involve the best consequences on balance for everyone concerned – *but* it involves treating one person in a way that violates principles of justice and dignity. If you consider that this policy must be ruled out, then you are recognising the principles of justice and dignity as ethically fundamental. Appeals to human rights are examples of principles functioning in this kind of way; they are meant to outweigh appeals to consensus or to the general consequences. In a metaphor from card games that some philosophers have used, human rights and perhaps some other fundamental principles can trump other considerations.

Hodgkinson refers to such principles as 'transrational'. We might take this to mean that reasons do not *need* to be given for them: in many contexts that will be true, because the people concerned will already accept some fundamental principles (we shall look below at a case in which an underlying concern for equality of opportunity seems to be accepted among the staff of a school). But that is different from saying that no reasons *can* be given for it. Hodgkinson sometimes seems to be saying that the highest principles are beyond rational justification. This comes close to taking a subjectivist or an emotivist view of such principles, which, as mentioned above, is to say that if we decide to put weight on, say, a principle of equal opportunities, then ultimately this is just our preference. But that would be a surprising conclusion from someone who clearly – as his schema shows – wants to distinguish matters of principle from preferences. And it would be an unsettling conclusion for education, since it means that if, for instance, you encounter people who say they do not care about equal opportunities, you cannot give them any reasons why they should take equal opportunities seriously.

Though it may be difficult to give further argument for fundamental ethical principles – partly because many people are not used to thinking in that way – that does not mean it is impossible. To religious believers there may be arguments available that depend ultimately on the existence of God, but for obvious reasons not everyone will accept such arguments. Philosophers have offered a variety of secular arguments – which means in this context, not that the arguments depend on denying the existence of a God, but simply that they do not depend on accepting God's existence; they are arguments that do not use religious discourse at all. To try to give firm arguments for a range of fundamental principles – and to consider objections to the arguments – would take us too far into moral philosophy for the purposes of this book. But in at least some cases a rational justification does not seem too hard to find.

In the case of equal opportunities, we could argue as follows. Where there is any selection to be done – for example, of staff for positions or of students for access to courses – then *discrimination* takes place in an ethically neutral sense of the term, where 'discrimination' simply means 'differentiating according to criteria'. Such discrimination is rational when it is made consistently according to criteria that are relevant to the matter in hand; if the discrimination rests on irrelevant criteria then it is irrational and thereby unjustified. If, for instance, places were being allocated on an advanced course in philosophy, then having taken a preliminary course in the subject, or having shown interest and aptitude in it, would be relevant factors. Ethnicity, gender, physical disability and so on would be irrelevant. So to make the selection in a way that gives weight to these irrelevant factors would be irrational.

It may be said that being able to give a rational justification for a principle such as equality of opportunity does not show an educational leader or anyone else what they actually need to do to put it into practice. That is true. Understanding why we should hold a principle in the first place *may* give us a clearer view of what it is we are trying to achieve and in that way may help, but in any concrete situation there will always be many considerations to take into account besides the principle itself. (For a discussion of how the leadership of a school may try to put equal opportunities into practice see Coleman (2002).)

Apart from having a clear view of the principle in question, educational leaders need to take as clear a view as they can of the likely consequences of their decisions (because, for instance, a strategy that might appear to have good consequences in terms of equal opportunities could also have less desirable side effects), and they need to consider how far there can be a consensus in the school about a given strategy (partly out of respect for the other people concerned, and partly because lack of consensus may itself tend towards undesirable consequences). Even if Hodgkinson is right in putting certain fundamental principles in a different category from values grounded in consequences or in consensus, it certainly does not follow that consequences and consensus can be neglected. Actually it is debatable whether those principles should be in a quite separate category. To refer to the consequences of following a principle is, on the face of it, a rational way of justifying it; indeed for utilitarianism it is ultimately the only way that a principle can be justified. And where a principle is one that, if it is to make a difference in practice, must be followed by everyone in some group, then to appeal to a consensus also seems rational. Indeed it is possible to combine considerations of both kinds within one theory. For instance, the German theorist Jürgen Habermas (1990) has developed an approach he calls discourse ethics or communicative ethics, which holds that norms are justified only when they can meet with the approval of all those who would be subject to the consequences of their application.

The points made in the last few paragraphs are about the *justification* of principles. The question of *motivation* is a different one, since very few human beings are motivated purely by considerations of rationality (and people who were motivated solely in that way would not necessarily be very nice people to know). Since the question of why people are – or are not – motivated by fundamental principles seems to be a question about individuals, I shall come back to it in Chapter 3 when focusing on the qualities of individuals in leadership roles. For the moment, as a prelude to the following chapters, it will be helpful to look at the variety of ways in which values can make a difference in educational leadership.

How do values make a difference in education?

The following case study is one in which equality of opportunity is clearly important, but is by no means the only value that features in the case or that may be relevant to your thinking about it. The case, supplied by Derek Glover, shows something of the concrete complexity of leadership activities within schools.

Case study: Red Meadow School

The starting point here is action research within Red Meadow Junior School into gender differences in achievement. The material for this has emerged from senior staff consideration of pupil achievement and the use of Cognitive Ability Test results on entry and an attempt to see whether pupils are performing at their potential level. The identification of discrepancies led the staff to a consideration of the ways in which their attitudes to boys and girls differed. At Red Meadow this was an uncomfortable process because it touched many staff on a raw nerve. The school, formerly a traditional primary school serving an area of white population, had developed its ethos from that origin. There was high respect for learning, strong competitive sport for the boys and musical activities for the girls, ability grouping arrangements for all years and a curriculum that favoured the more academic pupils. All were expected to wear the school uniform: pinafore dresses and blouses for the girls and short trousers and shirts for the boys. Parents had reported difficulty in securing willing acceptance of the uniform by the boys because it was 'old fashioned'.

When the staff met to consider the emerging disparity between boys' and girls' achievements at the end of their time in the school, the immediate observation from a group of male staff was that 'the boys need to be kicked into action ... the school has got too soft'. This was challenged by two of the younger female staff who urged that 'not all boys are the same and some need more gentle encouragement' and 'there are some for whom the macho image creates considerable unhappiness'. When the battle lines had thus been drawn it was clear that there were underlying problems. These included resentment by the women staff that most of the men took part in inter-school staff cricket or football matches on Friday evenings and then adjourned to a local bar with the male deputy headteacher, a feeling that the girls were always put into the situation of 'doing the housekeeping bit for any school activity', and that 'there is more to life than academic success and some boys and girls need to be recognised for their social and creative skills'. It was noted that the boys were only encouraged on the sports field if they were capable in the classroom.

The headteacher was aware that some constructive way forward had to be found and gained the agreement of staff to the use of an attitudinal survey that had been developed to test opinion on the way in which girls and boys were treated within a community. The aim of this was to see whether the school was really doing what the parents wanted and was giving an education appropriate to the changing conditions in a more ethnically mixed area. On the basis of the report the head proposed that the values of the school should be re-examined and that only when that had been satisfactorily achieved could strategies for improvement for all pupils be suggested. A technique of 'smiley faces' was also used to gain some picture of the level of happiness of boys and girls.

The reports showed that the girls and their parents perceived that they were fulfilling gender stereotypes and that the attitudes of male staff were such that the girls felt embarrassed by the way in which the boys were treated. It was a surprise to a hard core of male staff when the results from boys and their parents showed that they felt they were treated in a rough way by many male staff and indulged by some female staff. Possibly more likely to affect long-term results was the fact that both boys and girls objected to the way in which their working groups within classes were separated into boys and girls by ability at the start of each term, and that any attempt to integrate the groups or change their composition was resisted by most staff. In the words of one eight-year-old boy 'once you are in your group (Lions, Tigers and Leopards for the boys, Gazelles, Antelopes and Zebu for the girls) you are there for good, so what's the use of trying?', and of one girl: 'there just is no way you can win because we have been told that girls are no good at arithmetic and that is that!'

After lengthy discussion between parents, staff, community representatives and the headteacher it was subsequently agreed that the common values of the staff of the school would be restated as:

- We value all pupils irrespective of ability, gender and individual personality.
- We recognise that the staff are the biggest influence on student attitude and determine to offer role models that are non-threatening and do not reinforce traditional stereotypes.
- We recognise that pupils change over time and agree to consider how we can provide greater flexibility in learning approaches and arrangements.
- We recognise that there is an entitlement curriculum for all pupils and that this should be experienced, as far as ability allows, irrespective of gender or handicap.

Identify the references to values that you find in this account. Which of these are the head or other teachers explicitly referring to in their own thinking and discussion? Are there other values influencing the school that the staff do not themselves identify?

This school is making an attempt to pay explicit attention to its values. We can see that one particular value, or interrelated cluster of values, lay behind the initial concern that led to discussion about the gender discrepancies. The school later expressed this value in the words 'We value all pupils irrespective of ability, gender and individual personality.' We might sum this up as the principle of equal respect. The final item in the school's statement of its values could be called a principle of equal opportunities. Indeed one could say that these four statements together amount to a strong statement of a concern with equality of opportunities.

Of course, there are other values referred to in this account. Given the nature of values – as conceptions of what is desirable – there is no correct answer to the question: 'How many values are referred to in this account?' What one person counts as two distinct values, another may count as two aspects or two ways of stating the same value. The first and the fourth items in the school's statement of values might be expressions of two values or of one. And what of the second and third items? Perhaps strictly speaking they are not statements of values. The second states a matter of fact – that the staff are the biggest influence on student attitude – and a commitment that the staff make, but in the process it certainly refers to the ideas – about what is desirable – that it is better to be non-threatening and to avoid traditional stereotypes. The third item again states a matter of fact – that pupils change over time – and recognises that flexibility is desirable. Even in the statements of fact, values are being expressed, since it is implied that these facts are important ones to take into account.

There are other values that are referred to by the author of the account but not – so far as we are told – by the staff . The mention of high respect for learning, strong competitive sport for the boys and musical acitivities for the girls shows some of the things that the school values (and also leaves it uncertain whether the value attached to the musical activities is as great as that attached to the competitive sport). The existence of school uniform must have something to do with the school's values; we are not told exactly what values underpin the policy of having a uniform, but we are shown in relation to uniform that there is some discrepancy between the school's policy and the attitudes of some of the boys.

The next paragraph shows that some of the teachers value a certain kind of masculinity on the part of the boys. For two of the female staff, if there is anything positive about this macho image at all, its value is certainly outweighed by the importance of the boys' happiness; they rate unhappiness as a very important *negative* consideration (in this respect they are agreeing, as it happens, with utilitarianism). Probably most if not all of the staff agree on the positive value of happiness, since they put some weight on the result of the 'smiley faces' exercise, but it may be that different teachers would make a different balance between the importance of the children's present happiness and the importance of their future 'success' in life.

Other values emerge in the account that are nowhere directly expressed. It appears that the head values the opinions of the staff. Either the head, or the staff generally, think it is worthwhile to spend time in discussion with parents and community representatives. One could say that the school is making an effort to be democratic in the process by which it arrives at its new statement of values (though the pupils are apparently involved only indirectly, being consulted but not actually joining in the discussions). This effort may seem, however, to be coming rather late. It appears that there has not prior to this exercise been ongoing discussion between the staff; the ethos of the school seems to have been set largely by some of the male staff.

The school's new statement of values acknowledges that all are in principle valued equally and that attention will be paid to individual needs. On the other hand, it does not indicate that there will be any change in future in the way that school policy is arrived at and put into practice. This leaves it unclear how far the practices of the school actually will change in line with its new set of stated values.

Even on this, relatively superficial, analysis the account shows something of the complexity of the issues of values that a headteacher has to take into account. Values have to enter into the head's thinking in a number of ways. There are some relatively long-term aims to which the school is committed (academic success appears to be an important aim for this school). On the other hand, if some of the children are actually being made unhappy now by their experiences in the school, this fact may be allowed to put some constraints on the way the aims are pursued.

One thing we are not directly told about is the personal qualities of the head. The head is aware that a constructive way forward has to be found. It is not very clear whether the head is proactively leading the school in the direction of greater equality of opportunity rather than responding to events at a time when problems are emerging. No doubt someone who actually knew this headteacher would be in a better position to comment on their qualities as a leader.

We can finish this section by listing more systematically some of the ways in which values make a difference to decisions and actions.

- *Goals and purposes*. Values enter into our goals and purposes in action. When we act deliberately there is something we are aiming at. Sometimes what we are aiming at is to promote a certain value. So educational policy-makers may, for instance, be aiming to promote social justice. Perhaps more often, we are aiming at some complex state of affairs, and our values come into our judgements that this state of affairs rather than some alternative is the one we should be aiming at. We shall look further at goals and purposes in the next chapter.
- *Constraints on action*. Values can put constraints on what we do in order to achieve our goals. A good set of exam results for the whole school may be a valuable goal to aim at, but some ways of trying to achieve this goal – ways that involve falsifying the results, for example – may be ruled out.

- *Personal qualities.* Taking values into account in our actions, whether in setting goals or recognising constraints, is still not the only way in which we use values. It is also important to recognise that we appeal to values, implicitly or explicitly, when we make appraisals of persons. Suppose you think of one person as honest, fair-minded and generous, while another person might be dishonest, biased and mean. Then you are certainly working with values in the sense of our definition, i.e. conceptions of the desirable (it is desirable to be honest and fair-minded, undesirable to be dishonest and biased). But these are conceptions, not directly about what is to be done or not done, but about personal qualities. In Chapter 3 we shall look at the ways in which certain personal qualities may be important for educational leaders.
- *Qualities of organisations.* It is important to notice that we can attribute desirable or undesirable qualities to groups and organisations as well as to individuals. We can speak, for instance, of a caring school as well as of a caring person. We shall return in Chapters 5 and 6 to the question of what is involved in attributing desirable (or undesirable) qualities to a whole school.

Finally in this chapter, some cautionary notes about ways in which we should *not* think about values for educational leadership (drawing in part on Foster, 2003).

- We should not put all our reliance on empirically based approaches to thinking about values – looking at how people try to pursue their goals and to put their values into effect – because while such approaches can give us a sense of what is possible and show effective ways of achieving given ends, they cannot tell us which ends we *should* be pursuing.
- We should not expect that values can be handled by erecting a set of rules for educational leaders to follow. Values are not like that (and therefore this book will not attempt to give you a set of rules for good leadership).
- We should not think that looking into values in the context of educational leadership is entirely about looking at the values of individual leaders; we need to take into account the interpersonal and cultural contexts in which people in leadership roles are working.

Summary

This chapter has concentrated on understanding the nature of values and why values are important in educational leadership. Recognising that there is no definitive correct definition of values, I have tried to clarify the nature of values by asking you to reflect on your own understandings prior to reading this book and to examine these in the light of ideas in the literature.

You should now be in a position to see that our discussion in the following chapters will have to include:

- the way that values affect what we are aiming at – this will be a major theme in both Chapter 2, on educational aims and purposes, and Chapter 4, on vision in education;
- the way that some states of affairs can be incompatible with certain values – in Chapter 5, for instance, you will encounter an example of a school culture that seems clearly undesirable in the light of values of respect, equality and personal well-being;
- the way that we value not just states of affairs but also qualities of persons – Chapter 3 will ask whether we can identify desirable qualities of individual leaders, and Chapter 5 will look at desirable qualities of schools as organisations.

Suggested further reading

Begley, P. (2003) 'In pursuit of authentic school leadership practices', in Begley, P. and Johansson, O. (eds), *The Ethical Dimensions of School Leadership*. Dordrecht: Kluwer. A useful introduction to the field, including consideration of the nature of values and of Hodgkinson's contribution.

Blackburn, S. (2001) *Being Good: A Short Introduction to Ethics*. Oxford: Oxford University Press. A very accessible guide by a philosopher to thinking about values and ethics. Also published under the title *Ethics* in the Oxford University Press *Very Short Introductions* series.

Haydon, G. (2007) *Values in Education*. London: Continuum. Not focusing on leadership, but has more than the present book on the nature of morality.

Hodgkinson, C. (1991) *Educational Leadership: The Moral Art*. New York: State University of New York Press. As this chapter has indicated, Hodgkinson is perhaps the best known of writers on values in leadership and this is probably the best of his books for getting an overview of his position. Some brief extracts from this book are used in the next chapter.

Richmon, M. (2004) 'Values in educational administration: them's fighting words!', *International Journal of Leadership in Education*, 7 (4): 339–56. Combines an overview of the academic debates on values in leadership with a sympathetic but critical assessment of Hodgkinson.

2 | Educational aims and moral purpose

This chapter will look at the goals that leaders in education may be aiming at. We shall consider what can be said in general terms about the aims of education. We shall also ask in what sense we can expect educational leaders to be motivated by a sense of *moral purpose*, and we shall recognise that leaders have to pursue such a purpose within constraints imposed from outside the school itself.

This chapter will help you to:

- understand the value of explicit reflection on educational aims;
- be aware of a variety of commonly held views about the purposes of education;
- be aware in particular of a variety of moral or political aims in education;
- understand the idea of moral purpose in education;
- be aware of some of the difficulties in putting moral purpose into action.

There are four main sections in this chapter: the importance of aims and purposes; the diversity of educational purposes; moral and political aims in schooling; and moral purpose.

The importance of aims and purposes

One of the commonest ideas in recent research on schooling has been that of school effectiveness. It may seem obvious that part of the role of school leaders is to promote the effectiveness of their schools. It is vital to notice, though, that effectiveness is always relative to purposes. An individual or an organisation can be effective, or ineffective, in promoting certain ends. The value of being effective in a particular case must depend on the value of the ends.

For a chilling example, but one always worth remembering in a context of leadership, think of successful leaders within the Nazi Party during the Second World War. The success of these leaders was a matter of effectiveness in promoting Hitler's 'final solution'. Those who were less effective would have feared for their jobs and perhaps for their lives. But in that situation, ineffectiveness (relative to Nazi ends) was better, morally, than effectiveness; there were a few brave people, even within the ranks of the Nazi Party, who were deliberately and unobtrusively ineffective. That is to say, they were ineffective in promoting the Nazi Party's ends; in terms of saving lives or helping people retain some human dignity they may have been as effective as they could be. (If you know the book or the film *Schindler's List* you have a case study of someone maintaining the appearance of effectiveness as judged by those in authority while secretly being as effective as he could in pursuing more moral purposes.)

The general point here is that when we praise the effectiveness of leaders we normally mean that they are effective in promoting the goals of their organisation. In most cases we may assume that the goals of the organisation are themselves good – or at least not immoral – but we shouldn't take this for granted.

There may be some goals or aims that are shared by almost any organisation – for instance, almost any organisation seeks to maintain its own survival over time. But in other ways different organisations have different goals. If there are goals that are distinctively important in the context of schools, we would expect these to have something to do with the fact that the organisations concerned are educational ones.

At this point, then, we should ask in what ways educational organisations have goals or aims that may be distinctive from those of other organisations. The question is not just about the purposes that a society may *expect* education to serve, but also about how far we can give a justification for one purpose or another.

In what follows I shall not be making any systematic distinction between 'ends', 'goals', 'aims' or indeed 'purposes'. If you consider that there are significant differences between the meanings of these terms, you should use whichever you think is most appropriate in particular contexts. In this section I shall mostly use the term 'aims', because there is a body of literature – perhaps particularly associated with philosophy of education – that has discussed 'the aims of education'.

Despite that body of literature, it is – to quote John Dewey (1916: 107) – 'well to remind ourselves that education as such has no aims. Only persons, parents, and teachers, etc., have aims, not an abstract idea like education.'

Dewey is right that an abstract idea cannot have aims, but we do need to modify Dewey's claim so as to acknowledge that an institution or organisation can have aims. At least, it is an assumption of much of the literature about educational leadership and management that a school can have aims, not only particular individuals working within the school. You might wonder whether the aims of the school can be identified with the aims that the headteacher or principal has for the school; we shall come back to this question in a slightly different form when we look at the idea of vision in Chapter 4.

At this point it will be helpful if you reflect on your aims and the aims of the institution within which you work. We shall start with a question about your aims as a teacher, because although many teachers do not have managerial or leadership roles, the majority of leaders in educational institutions either are still teachers or have been teachers. And there must be a sense in which those doing the teaching and those doing the management and leadership are engaged in the same activity – the activity of education – even if they are not actually the same people.

Ask yourself the following questions and make a note of your answers:

1. *What are your aims as a teacher? (Or what were your aims as a teacher when you had a direct teaching role?)*
2. *What are your aims as an educational leader/manager?*
3. *What are the aims of the school (or other educational institution) in which you work?*

You may be able to answer question 3 by referring to an actual document which sets out the aims of your school. If your school does have such a document, there are two further questions:

(a) *How was this stated set of aims arrived at? (Was it formulated by one person? Arrived at collaboratively?)*
(b) *Do you consider that the document is an accurate statement of what the people working in the school really are aiming at, or are there any discrepancies?*

One final question asks you to look over the answers you have given to questions 1–3 and see how far they match each other.

4. *Are your aims as a teacher, your aims as a leader within your school and the aims of the school itself the same? If not, what are the differences and what is the reason for these differences?*

There may well be some differences in the three sets of aims you have picked out above. For instance, teachers of a particular subject – and managers with responsibility for a particular subject – will have aims relating to the popularity and status of their subject within the school. The principal of the school will have aims relating to the quality and retention of staff, and so on. But there are also likely to be overlaps between the sets of aims, and it will surely be in these areas of overlap that the distinctively educational aims will be found.

Reflection on aims can seem rather abstract, but for school leaders it can raise very practical issues. The following case study (supplied by Derek Glover) shows how such issues might be played out in relation to a secondary school in Australia.

Case study: Blue Waters School

Blue Waters School is a five form entry secondary school for pupils of all abilities in a clearly defined rural town in South Australia. It has enjoyed good relationships with the local community and has benefited from considerable local financial help in preparing and then undertaking the development of an arts and leisure centre for joint use by the school and community. The Management Committee of the centre has been in place for nearly three years and is chaired by John Gray, the managing director of a local agricultural manufacturing company employing about eighty full-time staff. Julie Ferris, the headteacher, knows that at a local meeting John Gray has been outspokenly critical about the quality of applicants for vacancies at 16+ under the state apprenticeship scheme. However, she has asked him to be one of three speakers talking to parents and students as part of a symposium on 'Preparing for the Future – Our Way through the Careers Minefield'. The other two speakers invited are Dr Golightly, a representative of the University College in the state capital, and Mrs James, the local representative of the Community Health Trust.

The views expressed at the meeting can be summarised as follows:

John Gray

Greatly concerned about the way education is going. Students seem to be spending longer at school with no obvious return to either themselves, parents or employers. Students are now being prepared for examinations that are too easy because all the course work is done first and the amount of retained and applied knowledge is reduced. There seems to be no control over what is learned at school and there will be enormous problems because the able students are staying on at school and the least able are incapable of coping with the numeracy and literacy skills required by the working world – especially when they can't cope with mental arithmetic.

Dr Golightly

Not terribly worried about the issues raised by the first speaker because local industry is now getting considerable financial support to put reorganised apprenticeship schemes into place. In his view we should be aiming to provide all students with the key skills that will enable them – and the country – to survive. Would not press for any return to the computational basics of a bygone age, but does regret that so much of the time when a young person first goes to college is spent in socialisation skills, preparation for individual learning and helping the student settle into new routines and regimes. Wants more general education for most students and later decision-making to avoid good material going into local unchallenging employment at too early a stage.

Mrs James

Considers that the earlier speakers were commenting from their own narrow needs. She believes in school as a preparation for life in the community and is much more concerned that students should understand what the world is about. This could then lead to a reduction in teenage parenting, to less inappropriate and unhappy placing in jobs, and to some enhancement of personal self-esteem. Students should be being groomed for success and not spend their formative years jumping through hoops.

These divergent views set Julie Ferris thinking about the rationale, processes and purposes of the curriculum offered by her school. Conversations with the senior management team were not totally successful because they seemed incapable of separating the messages from the messengers. Julie was not prepared to accept this as a viewpoint because she wanted the staff to look at what was being done to move away from the subject-based view of the curriculum to a 'curriculum for life'. Her immediate thought was that she should prescribe the curriculum to be offered, but her gut feeling was to look at the needs of the young people and then to negotiate with all parties to secure a curriculum that would match the needs of her pupils in the twenty-first century. The staff felt that such negotiation would be an admission that she was not leading, and they expressed the view that they would be happy to settle for 'an old-fashioned package of subjects' if only she would accept that she couldn't change the world.

What would you do if you were in Julie Ferris's situation?

This headteacher has her own view about how to proceed, but she also faces conflicting demands both from members of the local community and from her own staff. Her decision about her next move would have to be made in the light of her own understanding, from experience, of these circumstances.

At the same time, since she is in a leadership role you may think that she should not just be responding to surrounding pressure and demands. She may engage in a more general reflection about the demands that society makes on schools and about the relationship between different kinds of aims for education.

In reading the more general reflections on educational purposes that follow here, ask yourself whether such reflections would be useful to you in your own leadership role.

The diversity of educational purposes

In the first chapter I mentioned how influential Christopher Hodgkinson has been in the literature on values in educational leadership. In one of his works (1991: 23–6), discussing what he calls 'The constellation of purposes', he divides the purposes of education into three strands, often in practice interwoven. These are indicated in the three following quotations:

Aesthetic education

By the aesthetic purposes of education are meant those ends primarily associated with self-fulfilment and the enjoyment of life. Much falls within this rubric. The basic curriculum remains that of the liberal arts and the humanities but it can also be said to include the tool subjects of literacy and numeracy as well as much of the content of adult education. Sports and the entertainment arts are likewise means to the aesthetic ends of education. (pp. 23–4)

Economic education

All vocational education or training is economic in motivation. In crudest terms people undertake this sort of education with the manifest aim of making money ... while the first days of schooling may be construed as aesthetic wherein the aim is to impart initial literacy and numeracy to the learner, still this aim is also instrumental and prerequisite to further progress throughout the structured educational system and thus to the ultimate economic status of the learner. (p. 24)

Ideological education

It has always been a function of education to transmit the culture of society in which it occurs ... The thrust of this purposive aspect of education extends into all levels of educational structure although perhaps with a major emphasis in the earlier years of the educational process. As has been said apocryphally of Catholic educators, the principle seems to be, 'Give me the first years of a child's life and I will give you the man'. (p. 25)

It would be surprising if all discussions of educational purposes divided up the field in just the same way. In Bottery's (1990) discussion, for instance, there are four models of education, distinguished chiefly by the emphasis on certain purposes. These are:

• the cultural transmission model;
• the child-centred model;
• the social reconstruction model;
• the 'GNP code' (GNP = Gross National Product).

While it is inevitable that different writers will categorise the range of educational purposes in different ways using different labels, it is possible to identify many common factors. All sources, for instance, are likely to recognise that any actual education system in the modern world has among its purposes to provide a workforce with knowledge and skills that will serve the economy. (In Bottery's scheme these purposes are covered by the 'GNP code'.)

The idea of 'cultural transmission' is also present in most discussions, though in Hodgkinson this purpose may come partly under 'aesthetic education' and partly under 'ideological'. What is to be included under cultural transmission may be far from obvious. What people often see as a major purpose of formal education or schooling is not to transmit all of a society's culture, or a random selection from it, but to transmit those parts which are perceived to be of most value – which may be in literature, sciences, the arts, etc.

Why is it important to transmit what is seen as most valuable in a society's culture? The answer may seem obvious, but it is worth recognising that cultural transmission may be valued both for its importance to the society as a whole – since many of its cultural assets would be lost if they were not transmitted through education – and for the benefits it brings to individuals. Here we are talking about benefits that are not primarily economic; rather, the idea is that the lives of individuals are enriched through their knowledge and appreciation of what is culturally valuable. So this fits with the strand that Hodgkinson calls 'aesthetic education'.

This in turn is close to an idea which has often been called 'liberal education': an education which brings to the individual knowledge and understanding – of history, say, or of art – that are valued for their own sake. Such an education is seen as making a person's life more interesting, richer, more satisfying, even if it does not turn out to have instrumental value in promoting the individual's material conditions of life. This idea has been influential within philosophy of education, where it is especially associated with Richard Peters (1966).

Liberal education has often been contrasted with vocational education: equipping people to have an occupation, do a paid job. (Much of the rhetoric of education today from politicians and policy-makers almost takes it for granted that producing a skilled workforce is the primary point of education.) Vocational education (which may be a preparation for any sort of occupation, not just ones which involve a 'vocation' in the sense of some special calling) clearly serves economic ends: both those of society – which wants a well-trained workforce – and those of individual students and their parents, who may think of education primarily as a route to earning a living. Liberal education, in contrast, is seen as freeing individuals from thinking of what is worthwhile purely in economic or instrumental terms. Liberal education also is often associated with the idea that individuals should be able to think for themselves, make their own decisions and find their own way in life.

The idea of liberal education leaves open a range of possibilities for the curriculum. At one end of the spectrum, the idea of the kind of learning that is most valuable is taken from the traditions and the 'high culture' of the society. So students will be introduced to, say, Shakespeare and classical music in preference to soap opera and rock music, and also in preference to (or alongside) studies that are more directly useful. At the other end of the spectrum, it may be reckoned that nothing will really be of value to the individual unless the individual chooses it for its own sake. So a premium will be put on the interests and choices of children themselves (it is usually children rather than older students that advocates of this approach have in mind); this yields the 'child-centred' model that Bottery mentions.

So far in this brief survey of some possible educational aims we have looked at the ideas of education as promoting learning that is valuable for its own sake, and of education as developing knowledge and skills that will serve economic ends, both for the sake of the learners themselves and for the benefit of the wider society. A further important category of aims that we need to consider, which is especially relevant for this book, is the transmission or development of values. This enters into Hodgkinson's *ideological education*.

It is not surprising that the category of the transmission or development of values overlaps with other purposes, because any kind of education influences students' values. The transmission of culture seeks to influence values in that the culture of a society incorporates judgements about what is valuable. The teacher of Shakespeare is seeking to promote, not a value-free knowledge of Shakespeare, but knowledge along with a sense of what is valuable in the work. Something similar is true of any subject. The teacher of mathematics, for instance, will usually hope, not just that students acquire certain skills that they can choose to use or neglect, but that they realise the importance of these skills and acquire concerns for care and accuracy in mathematical procedures. The pursuit of economic aims also carries certain valuations about the importance of the economy and of productive work.

What of Bottery's social reconstruction? This is a purpose underpinned by a commitment to certain values. An idea of social justice is central, and the social reconstructionist view thinks that justice can be achieved only through quite radical change. Bottery points out that in the context of developed Western societies it may be questioned whether a radical reconstruction of society is needed. But there are, of course, other contexts in the world. Consider the following statement by the Director-General of UNESCO:

> Wars will not cease, either on the ground or in people's minds, unless each and every one of us resolutely embarks on the struggle against intolerance and violence by attacking the evil at its roots. Education offers us the means to do this. It also holds the key to development, to receptiveness to others, to population control and to the preservation of the environment. Education is what will enable us to move from a culture of war, which we unhappily know only too well, to a culture of peace, whose benefits we are only just beginning to sense. (Tedesco, 1994: 1, cited in Harber and Davies, 1997: 153)

Finding a way through the web of values

The aims pursued by schools and their leaders are not entirely up to individual schools, let alone individual persons. So any reflection on educational aims at this level will operate within constraints imposed by the wider system. We shall come back to this point later. Nevertheless, educational leaders surely need to have as clear a sense as they can of what it is they are trying to achieve. This is part of what it means to speak of leaders having a 'moral purpose' or 'a vision'. We shall come back to both of those ideas as well.

So far, you have seen something of the complexity of thinking about educational aims. But how are leaders to get any clarity of purpose when there are so many ideas about what schools should be aiming at? Reading, experience, reflection and discussion all seem to be vital; a few pages within this book will certainly not tell you what you should think. But here is just one suggestion – developed in Haydon (2007) – about how one might attempt to get the whole field into some sort of perspective.

Suppose we start by recognising that ultimately all of the questions about what education should be doing come down to questions about values: that is, questions about what is important in life, what matters most. At the broadest underlying level, the purpose of education is to improve people's lives in some way. (If education did nothing to improve anyone's life, why should we bother about it at all?) But of course, there is room for different interpretations of what makes for a better life, and for different emphases on one factor or another.

At this point we might begin very roughly to put the things that are important in life on some sort of scale from the most basic to the less basic. At the most basic level, sheer survival is important, and then such considerations as freedom from injury and disease, a sense of security, adequate nutrition and shelter. We may consider that a society that is functioning well will be providing such things for its members, but they cannot be guaranteed; and there are many things that people can be taught that may help them to achieve these important things (hygiene, nutrition, skills enabling people to support themselves). So schools can be important in trying to promote and maintain what may be seen as the most basic values. But there is also a traditional way of thinking that associates education with a different range of considerations that have more to do with 'the life of the mind'. On this view – the liberal education mentioned above – education has been seen as concerned with knowledge and understanding, rationality and more elaborated and refined kinds of appreciation of the natural world and of human creations.

A lot of debate about educational aims has in effect been about the priorities to be allotted to these different sorts of considerations. (And to repeat, that makes the debate one about values, since it is about what is important in life.) To see it as a question of priorities or balance is clearly right, since these different kinds of goods are dependent on each other for their realisation. It is clear that most people will not get far in the more elaborated kinds of understanding and appreciation of the world if their basic needs are not satisfied, but it is also the case that the continuing achievement of good health, nutrition, security and so on depends on people being able to exercise a whole range of skills and knowledge, including not least the technological and scientific.

Let's try to tie all this together by emphasising two points. The first is that in the modern world a degree of specialisation, and hence a degree of reliance on the skills and knowledge of others, is unavoidable. However good our educational endeavours, we cannot hope to equip every individual with all the skills and knowledge which will provide for their every need throughout life. We should remember this in the context of reflection on educational aims. It used to be widely thought that the aims of education would reflect the specialisation within life. Some people would be rulers and some would be followers, so there would be different educational aims for the elite and for the masses. Some people – mostly men – would be breadwinners and some – mostly women – would look after homes. So there would be different educational aims for boys and for girls. And so on.

Today – though still more in some parts of the world than others – we tend to start the discussion of educational aims from a much more egalitarian basis. In some way, we assume, the aims of education are the same for everyone. (When a school sets out its aims in print, it is unlikely to divide this up into one list of aims for one category of students and a different list for another category.) This assumption of the same aims for everyone is itself an important commitment which underlies much of our contemporary concern for equal opportunities in education (see Chapter 1 for an argument underpinning the importance of equal opportunities). But we should remember that having the same fundamental aims for everyone's education does not mean that we expect everyone to end up with just the same outcome. Different people can live valuable and productive lives in different ways and our educational aims have to recognise and respect this.

The second point that helps to tie it all together is that, since we live together in communities, and are dependent on each other and indeed vulnerable to each other, we cannot avoid moral and political concerns about how we relate to each other.

Moral and political aims in schooling

All societies (from the Greece of Plato and Aristotle and the China of Confucius onwards) have sought through education to address their moral and political concerns, hoping that the people emerging from education will be good persons, good members of the community, good citizens. (Hodgkinson mentions these concerns under the heading 'ideological education', while acknowledging that this strand is intertwined with the others.) In the following sections I shall ask you to reflect on these under-lying moral and political purposes and how they are addressed within different educational systems.

In some systems the aim of forming morally good persons has been sub-sumed under religious education. This fact has reflected a strong belief in some cultures that morality has to be rooted in religion. The belief that a good religious upbringing is the foundation of a good moral upbringing is still active within faith schools, which aim to bring children up within a specific religious tradition. But many schools today are secular, and in some countries, including the USA and France, the whole public schooling system is secular. In such schools moral aims have to be pursued in a dif-ferent way.

Some countries include courses in ethics or morals explicitly in the cur-riculum of public schools. Where this happens, such courses may or may not overlap with courses that seek to promote good citizenship. In Britain, any attempt to locate where in the curriculum moral and political aims are pursued would have to mention not only citizenship but also PSHE (Personal Social and Health Education) and Religious Education.

In your own professional environment, what is the situation regarding the promo-tion of moral and political aims?

- *Are there courses of religious instruction? If so, are these compulsory or optional?*
- *Are there courses in morals or ethics?*
- *Are there courses in civics or citizenship?*
- *In what ways, apart from explicit courses in the curriculum, do you consider that moral and political aims are promoted in schools?*

There is room for differences of opinion about the desirability of having distinct parts of the curriculum to address moral and political aims. Some people would argue that such aims are better addressed simply through the ethos of the school and the example set by teachers. But anyone reflecting on how such aims are best addressed – and school leaders can hardly avoid such reflection – needs to get clearer on just what the aims are. It is easy to say that the aim is to produce good people and good citizens, but there is room for many interpretations of what this means.

Consider the following list of some possible moral and political aims. (You may think of others that you would wish to add to the list.) Reflect on which of these aims you would wish to endorse. When you have picked out the aims you would endorse, reflect further on whether the aims you have picked out are all compatible with each other.

- The aim is that young people should grow up respecting the traditions of their culture.
- The aim is that young people should grow up behaving in the way that most people in their society behave.
- The aim is that young people should do what they are told by those in authority.
- The aim is that young people should learn to think for themselves and make their own decisions about what to do.
- The aim is that young people should develop the capacity for care and concern for others.
- The aim is that young people should understand and tolerate other people's different values.
- The aim is that young people should have a sense of pride in their national identity.
- The aim is that young people should obey the law and be loyal to their country.
- The aim is that young people should be active participants in the affairs of their community.
- The aim is that young people should be critical of the powers that be and prepared to work for change.

Even brief reflection on this list suggests that there is a heavy responsibility on educational leaders who are aware of the influence their institutions can have on the values and commitments with which young people grow up. The responsibility is not just to find the most effective way of pursuing moral and political aims that are set elsewhere. Since such aims are always open to dispute and interpretation, leaders have to take responsibility for the particular moral and political aims that are being pursued, and therefore need to be able to reflect on the possible aims. The next section will attempt to give some guidance in this reflection.

Values education

Perhaps the moral aim that seems the most obviously desirable to the general public in most parts of the world is that young people should be taught to behave well. Of course, we cannot leave the matter at that, since behaving *well* is an evaluative notion; explicitly or implicitly, some standards are needed by which to evaluate what is *good* behaviour. Where do these standards come from? The obvious answer, in turn, is that they are the standards of the society in question, but that answer by itself is not adequate. We know that standards change over time, and since education, in teaching young people, is necessarily looking towards the future, it should not take it for granted that standards will remain static. It is not difficult to think of societies in which some of the standards that prevailed in a given generation were ones that a later generation would repudiate: racially divided societies, for instance, in which a minority was grossly discriminated against, or societies in which the position of women was widely assumed to be inferior. Values education needs to allow for standards to improve.

How can standards be open to change and improvement? This can happen when at least some people in society are prepared to reflect on the prevailing standards and criticise them if they merit criticism. So education, in its overall responsibility to society, should not be bringing people up blindly to accept the prevailing standards.

This is not only part of education's responsibility to society but also part of its responsibility to individuals. No standard of behaviour or general rule can determinate in advance exactly how an individual should respond to every situation that he or she will encounter in life. General standards of behaviour can conflict with each other (people may find themselves, for instance, in a situation where it is impossible to tell the truth without hurting someone), and any standard needs to be interpreted in specific situations. So individuals need to be brought up to be capable not only of reflecting on the general standards but also of thinking about the specific situations in which they find themselves and so deciding for themselves what is the best thing to do in the circumstances.

There are good reasons, then, for educating people so that they will be able to think for themselves about what they should do. But this is not yet the end of the story. To say that standards change and should not be immune from criticism is not to say that there should be no shared standards at all. To put the emphasis *solely* on individuals being able to think for themselves would be to risk some of the benefits that shared standards can bring. To have shared standards of behaviour – even if they are recognised as *not* the final word on how individuals behave – is to have at least some basis for relying on others. We can relate to other people with a degree of trust rather than constant caution if we believe that there are at least some standards of behaviour that they share with us.

So perhaps education should be *both* trying to promote a recognition of some shared standards *and* trying to develop in individuals the ability to think for themselves. These two aims are not incompatible provided we do not take the prevailing standards as set in stone. But that still leaves the question of how education is to derive its conception of the prevailing standards. In a plural society these standards cannot simply be read off from the way the majority of people actually behave. For one thing, people's behaviour does not always match their professed values, and it may be the task of education to encourage young people, not just to do what others in fact do, but to aspire to something better. Then again, if schools derive the standards they teach from the way the majority of people behave, this may be privileging the values of one sector of society – a dominant majority – over others.

What, then, are schools to do? Different societies have handled this issue in different ways, but one common way is to seek to achieve some form of consensus through actual dialogue between representatives of different groups in society. In England in the mid-1990s, for instance, a National Forum for Values in Education and the Community was convened, with the task of trying to agree on a set of values that were widely accepted across the whole community. It did indeed come to an agreed Statement of Values, which still exists as part of the documentation for the National Curriculum. Many other countries also have their own list of values; sometimes it is required by government that schools should seek to promote the values listed, sometimes, as in England, the list is more a resource for schools to use as they wish. The existence of such lists shows at least two things: that agreement across a plural society is possible, and that agreement does not remove the need for interpretation or the scope for debate. Items on an agreed list of values will inevitably be phrased in quite broad terms, such as 'we should understand and carry out our responsibilities as citizens' or 'we should respect religious and cultural diversity' (to take two examples from the English statement: see the National Curriculum website www.nc.uk.net, or Talbot and Tate, 1997). Such broadly conceived values are far from prescribing exactly how people should behave in concrete situations, but they do provide a reference point for an individual's own thinking and for discussion.

The points made about the need for interpretation of values are all the more important when we turn from issues of interpersonal behaviour to questions of citizenship. In some countries or traditions of thought, being a good citizen is understood as little more than behaving well, conforming to society's norms. That is an unfortunate narrowing of the idea of citizenship, because life as a member of one of today's complex plural societies introduces issues that have to be worked through at a public level. That is true, for instance, of several of the items in the list of possible aims above. That young people should grow up respecting the traditions of their culture may be desirable, but in a multicultural society harmonious relations with other cultures have to be part of the aim as well. That people should have a sense of pride in their national identity may be an admirable aim, but on an international level this aim can lead to problems if the distinction is lost between pride in a distinct identity and the kind of nationalism that carries with it hostility to people with other identities. That people should obey the law and be loyal to their country may also be desirable but not if it precludes criticism of the law or of the powers that be. Citizenship, in short, demands much more of individuals, in terms particularly of their capacity for critical thinking, than conformity to social norms. Preparing young people for citizenship is one of the most important, and also probably one of the most demanding, roles that schools need to take on.

Moral purpose

The reflections so far on the purposes of education, and the place of moral and citizenship concerns within those purposes, can help you see why an important idea in some recent writing about educational leadership has been *moral purpose*.

- *What does the idea of 'moral purpose' convey to you?*
- *What does it mean to say that education has a moral purpose? What does this tell you about exactly what the purpose is, or is not?*
- *What does it mean to say that an educational leader has a moral purpose? What does this tell you about what that person is aiming at, and about what their motivation is?*

Your answers to the questions above will depend partly on what you understand by the term 'moral': different people do in fact use this word in rather different ways. What follows is my own sense of what the term 'moral purpose' conveys.

First, the purposes pursued in schools clearly should not be *immoral*; they must not actually violate any fundamental moral principles. Perhaps in most circumstances it is unlikely that any school would be pursuing immoral purposes, but it is not impossible. Imagine a situation in which the headteacher of a private school is also a businessman who owns the school. He might be running the school as a profit-making business. This would not generally be considered immoral in itself (except by radical anti-capitalists), but if his sole purpose were to maximise his profits regardless of any other considerations then we might well think this purpose immoral, because it would be treating other people, including the staff and students, simply as instruments in the pursuit of his own ends. (Not treating people solely as means to your own ends is an important moral principle associated with the philosopher Kant. It is one way of interpreting the idea of respect for persons, which you will encounter again in later chapters.)

Secondly, there is, of course, more to having a moral purpose than just avoiding immoral purposes. Recall that in Chapter 1 we considered what makes an issue an ethical or moral one. Two of the points were that:

- Moral or ethical matters seem to be about how people are treated – how people behave towards each other.
- While moral values, like other values, are conceptions of the desirable, they often seem to be more than just that. We may want to say, for instance, that being kind rather than cruel is not just *desirable* – it is

obligatory. We have the idea that morality is *binding* on people in ways that other conceptions of the desirable are not.

Education is a matter of some people – the teachers and educational leaders – deliberately exercising influence over others – the students. (The next chapter will consider the question of the teacher's authority that is raised by this fact.) This already makes it a matter to which judgements of what is morally good or bad can apply. And treating people in one way rather than another – especially when the people concerned are vulnerable, as children are in relation to adults – is not just a matter of preference. There are obligations involved here. Society owes it to its young people to bring them up and teach them in desirable ways (that is why we say that children have a *right* to education, not just that it would be a good thing for children to receive an education). So the purpose of education is one that society has a duty to pursue, and society puts much of the responsibility for pursuing that purpose onto schools.

Schools are not the only institutions that have responsibilities towards particular people, discharged on behalf of the wider society. We might say, for instance, that hospitals have such responsibilities, at least within a health service that is publicly run and funded. But there is a further point about the purposes of schools. Schools that are concerned with the general education of young people – unlike, say, a driving school or a swimming school – are trying to promote learning that is not ethically neutral. They cannot avoid, for better or worse, having an influence on the values, including the moral values, of young people; therefore they must do their best to influence these values for the better. This is a further dimension in which the purpose of schools is rightly considered a moral purpose.

Finally, yet a further point is introduced when we think of the purposes, not of education in general, but of the individuals involved in education. This is a point about the reasons or motives for which individuals do what they do. Many people expect that educators will not be motivated only by their own satisfaction – whether material or emotional – but that they will have the interests of young people at heart. Their own motivation will essentially be not selfish or egoistic, but *altruistic*. We will explore this idea of altruistic motivation further in the next chapter, drawing on a discussion by Peter Gronn (2003). For the moment there are two points worth making.

First, while the motivation behind people's work may be an important question in relation to any teacher, it is especially important for educational leaders. A teacher of mathematics, say, who does not really have the welfare of young people at heart, who is not concerned with their broader educational development and who professionally is merely trying to keep his salary coming in until retirement may nevertheless have some success in teaching mathematics. But we may question whether a school principal who is simply trying to do what the system requires so as to keep the job

40   *Values for educational leadership*

and earn the salary, without any broader altruistic motivation, can be a good leader. Many of the ideas in the next chapter on the qualities of individual leaders, and in the following chapter on vision, will be relevant to this question.

Second, an altruistic motivation can take different forms. Some leaders may be motivated by a strong sense of *caring* for the people in their charge (see Nias, 1999 for relevant research from primary schools in England, and Noddings, 1992 for a view of education built around caring, to which we shall return in Chapter 4). For others, an altruistic or moral motivation may be a matter not so much of personal concern for others as of following moral principles, such as an ideal of social justice. We shall look again in the next chapter at how such principles can function and how they may be justified.

Fullan on moral purpose

Michael Fullan, who is based in Canada and whose writing about leadership is set in a North American context, has probably done more than any other academic to bring the idea of moral purpose into the discourse of educational leadership. Fullan emphasises the importance of a 'strong sense of moral purpose'. The following quotation is representative:

> ... principals are constantly experiencing overload and a proliferation of expectations. This is a system problem, to be sure, but it is far more damaging if principals lose track of their moral compass. Why did I become an educator in the first place? What do I stand for as a leader? What legacy do I want to leave? ... These are all-important questions that should be continually revisited; otherwise the principal's role becomes overloaded with emptiness. (Fullan, 2003: 19)

However, Fullan's concern is not just with stressing the need for a moral compass or a sense of moral purpose; he wants to know how this can be put into action. It is not enough just to have the moral compass (which points the direction to be followed); you have to be able to see in practice how to move consistently in that direction. Fullan considers how in practice principals may successfully or unsuccessfully pursue their moral purpose at the school level. He considers a number of examples in which the school principal does have some sense of moral purpose, but fails to take it seriously enough or follow it through well enough.

Some attempts, he says, are only at a surface level, 'where what is being proposed sounds good and has all the right concepts, where leaders can talk a good game and even mean it, but where the ideas never get implemented with consistency or integrity'. (And it is not difficult for this to happen, given the 'overload and proliferation of expectations' already mentioned.)

Then there are cases, Fullan suggests, where the moral purpose goes only about 25 per cent below the surface. He cites a case in which the school leadership 'spend one day each month focused on literacy instruction' and 'a full day of professional development each month focused on developing nine leadership competencies the Central Administration has identified'. It is not too difficult to see why this initiative does not go to sufficient depth. The programme seems too mechanical and compartmentalised, as if one day a month focused on this and one day a month focused on something else (a predetermined list of competencies drawn up by Central Administration) could by itself achieve significant change. Fullan comments:

> Don't get me wrong: this is moral purpose, and many children are benefiting. But it is not very deep, may not last, and does not go nearly far enough in conceptualising the moral role of the principal.

Fullan goes on to give examples of schools which he judges are working at least at 50 per cent depth in effectively pursuing moral purpose. There are several factors which make a difference to a school's effectiveness in pursuing a moral purpose. Some factors are more or less technical: ways and means have to be worked out and implemented. Once put into practice, measures have to be followed through consistently.

Some factors are to do with personnel. If possible, Fullan implies, the principal has to select the right teachers or get teachers who are not the right people 'off the bus'. (For another perspective, from England, about a leader's possible need to shed staff, see Day et al. (2000: 146–9).) Short of the actual dismissal of staff, there is a message here about the importance of staff development. But there is still in the background the factor of a personal commitment to moral purpose. One principal is quoted as saying:

> I feel a moral responsibility to a child who is innocent and vulnerable in this society to try – at least in my little neck of the woods – to give them a good taste of America.

Aims and purposes within the broader system

No school principal is completely free to set his or her own purposes; all are subject to the 'proliferation of expectations' many of which will come from government, either regional or national.

Politicians and government agencies have their own views on the purposes of education, and these will not necessarily coincide with the views of school heads or principals (or with the views of teachers, parents or students). Think again of the different purposes distinguished by Hodgkinson or Bottery. Government will often give high priority to economic purposes. Students and their parents in some cases will give priority to the acquisition of skills that are valuable in the workplace. But at the same time many teachers, including many of those who have gone on to take up leadership roles, take a broader view of the aims of education, wanting their schools to develop well-rounded persons and citizens.

This point has, of course, often been noticed by writers on school leadership. William Foster (2003), cited in Chapter 1, referred to an earlier positivist or technicist view of educational administration (in the American sense of the term) according to which the policy-makers set the aims for schools and the administrator merely puts them into effect. This model of school leadership is still with us, and is perhaps often favoured by the politicians and government agencies. Indeed Wright (2001) goes so far as to refer to 'bastard leadership' as a common condition.

The idea that school leaders should be simply putting into effect the purposes set by the government is not easy to reconcile with the stress of writers such as Fullan on moral purpose within the school, unless we can assume that school leaders will always agree with the government on the purposes of education. But if we are to take seriously the idea that educators are professional people who are capable of thinking for themselves we surely cannot and should not make that assumption. At the same time, we can recognise that if school leaders are indeed able professional people they will have the capacity to work within government policy without slavishly following it. Leaders have to make decisions in the light of the conditions applying at particular times and places and these conditions can never be anticipated in detail at the level of policy. When leaders decide how best to put a policy into effect in their particular circumstances, they are inevitably using their professional judgement in interpreting the policy. Any policy which allows space for leadership at all must, then, allow some space for interpretation. This means there is still some room – though exactly how much will vary from one educational system to another – for particular schools and their leaders to put their own stamp on their pursuit of educational purposes.

Recognising this broader context, we can go on now to ask in the next chapter whether there are specific conditions and qualities that make it possible for an educational leader to pursue moral purpose successfully.

Summary

In this chapter we have looked at a number of questions about educational aims and purposes (without making any systematic distinction between the two terms). We considered a number of purposes for education that are widely recognised both by theoretical writers and within society, and we looked at ways in which, by thinking about the values underlying these purposes, we might be able to see them as not fundamentally conflicting. We gave particular attention to moral and political aims, since these explicitly involve values.

We examined the idea of moral purpose with particular reference to the work of Fullan, and recognised that the wider society puts constraints on the extent to which an individual leader can pursue his or her own sense of moral purpose.

We shall return to a similar theme in Chapter 4 under the heading of 'vision'. Before that, in Chapter 3, we shall look at the characteristics of individuals as leaders.

Suggested further reading

Dewey, J. (1916) *Democracy and Education*. New York: Macmillan. Chapter 8, 'Aims in education' is still a good introduction to thinking about the aims of education.

Fullan, M. (2003) *The Moral Imperative of School Leadership*. Thousand Oaks, CA: Corwin Press (Sage). A short book, which aims to inspire as well as to be practical. While very clearly rooted in its North American context, it is a good basis for thinking about moral purpose in education.

Haydon, G. (2007) *Values in Education*. London: Continuum. Contains a chapter on aims in education and more on the aims of moral education in particular.

Richmon, M. (2004) 'Values in educational administration: them's fighting words!', *International Journal of Leadership in Education*, 7 (4): 339–56. In criticising the relativist tendencies he finds in Hodgkinson, Richmon is effectively renewing a call for leaders to be driven by a moral purpose without being distracted by theoretical doubts about values.

3 | The individual leader

The last chapter concluded with a question about what can make it possible for an individual leader successfully to pursue his or her sense of moral purpose.

In later chapters we will look at views that see the pursuit of educational purposes as the responsibility of a whole institution within which leadership may be distributed across many persons. But the idea that leadership within one organisation or institution resides in one person is still a strong one in most cultures. At least as a historical legacy, the 'great man theory' of leadership is still with us. (The gender bias in the name of this theory is, of course, deliberate, since historically it has usually been men who have been held to have the qualities of a great leader. A few female figures with a similar reputation – such as Cleopatra, Queen Elizabeth I of England, Catherine the Great – stand out because they are exceptions.) The idea that leadership is about the activities and qualities of rather special individuals, and even the gender stereotypes that went with that idea, have by no means evaporated, as you will see in this chapter.

This chapter will help you to

- understand how a distinction can be made between power and authority, and what kinds of basis authority can have;
- be able to reflect on how far being a leader is a matter of being a certain sort of person;
- understand that there is a difference between following a principle and having a virtue;
- be able to discuss how we might identify which virtues are important in a leader.

This chapter has four main sections: authority in leadership; characteristics of the good leader; principles in leadership; virtues in leadership.

Within the educational literature, much of what has been written on the qualities of the individual leader is very positive in tone, emphasising the desirable attributes that can make for a successful school principal. Much of it, also, draws on experience in Britain and North America. But for this chapter we start with a view from Africa that calls attention to the very real problems that can arise when the effectiveness of schools is seen as turning almost entirely on the role of the individual leader.

Clive Harber and Lynn Davies have studied school leadership in several African countries, especially Ghana and Botswana. Based on these studies, their book on *School Management and Effectiveness in Developing Countries* (Harber and Davies, 1997) has a chapter with the intriguing title '"Leadership": headteacher as taxi driver'. One might interpret this title metaphorically – a matter of the head having the responsibility to deliver the members of the school to their destination or goal – but the authors' account shows that as a metaphor this would not be very appropriate. A taxi driver, after all, takes his or her passengers where they want to go; by this metaphor the head would be the servant of the school. That *is* a possible conception of the role of leader, as we shall see later in this chapter, but it is not the kind of leadership Harber and Davies found in their studies. In Botswana the head tended (this was in the 1990s) to have almost the sole responsibility, within the directives of government policy, for all aspects of the day-to-day running of the school. This put him (again the pronoun is deliberate, reflecting the dominant local tradition and practice) in a position of considerable power over all the staff of the school; it made it possible for the head to be, in Harber and Davies's term, a despot. It also gave him opportunities to supplement his income. Most of the staff in the rural areas did not have their own transport; heads sometimes had a vehicle that they could use to get supplies from the nearest town. The 'taxi driver' head, for a fee, drove his teachers into town on pay day so that they could do their shopping.

Harber and Davies's case studies help to put individual leadership into perspective by showing what it can amount to in concrete situations, especially outside the affluent countries in which most of the academic research into school leadership has been conducted. The evidence reported by these authors forms part of their case for moving away from a reliance on individual leadership towards a more democratic model.

No model of leadership makes the qualities shown by individuals irrelevant to good leadership and management; there is still a need to focus, as we are in this chapter, on what qualities it is desirable for leaders to have. But we also need to look at the role of an individual leader. What makes a headteacher a despot, to use Harber and Davies's word, may be partly a matter of the qualities shown by the individual but is also partly a matter of the role in which the individual is placed.

A leader needs some sort of authority, but need not have the power of a despot. So our next question in this chapter is about how we can distinguish legitimate authority from despotic power.

Authority in leadership

First, it is clear that if a leader is to be able to pursue a moral purpose, he or she needs to have the *authority* to do this. It is worth looking further into the nature of the authority that the leader can hold. When we say that someone has authority, an issue about values is already implicit; here we need to make that issue explicit. In everyday discourse authority is not always distinguished from power, but it helps to bring out the value issue if we make that distinction.

We can define *power* roughly as the ability of A (which may be an individual or an organisation) to get B to do what A intends B to do. There is a sense in which this definition is value-neutral; there is nothing in the definition to say whether it is a good or a bad thing that A is getting B to do something that A intends B to do. Whether it is good or bad will be decided by circumstances that are not captured in the definition. Suppose that as a teacher you see one child (A) bullying another (B); specifically, A by the threat of force gets B to hand over a ball that B has been playing with. Then A is exercising power over B, but is doing wrong in exercising this power. Suppose that you tell A to stop the bullying, and that A does stop. Then you have exercised power over A, but you were probably quite right to do this – you were acting within your authority.

What the notion of authority helps us to do is to distinguish between right and wrong exercises of power. A has no authority to tell B to hand over the ball; you, as a teacher, do have the authority to tell A to stop bullying B. 'Authority', then, is a value-loaded concept; roughly, it equals 'legitimate power'.

Not surprisingly, as with many value-loaded concepts, the situation is actually more complicated than this, but the idea of authority as legitimate power gives us a starting point in thinking about how authority relates to leadership. The exercise of power in human societies is very widespread and probably quite inevitable; almost anyone may be involved in the exercise of some power over somebody at some time (the twentieth-century French theorist Foucault has become particularly associated with the idea that power is very widely distributed). But, of course, some people have more power at their disposal than others. Leaders could not be leaders without the possibility of exercising some power (remember that in the value-neutral sense this only means that leaders are able to get other people to do what the leaders intend them to do), but if people are trying to exercise power over us we want to know if they are entitled to do that. When we recognise someone as a leader, we recognise that their exercise of power is legitimate; that is we recognise that they have, not just power, but authority over us. (What I mean here by 'recognising someone as a leader' is not a matter of applying the term 'leader' in an external, observer's way. Of course we can refer to Hitler as leader (*Führer*) of the Nazis without saying that his power was legitimate. But the point is that the people in Germany in the 1930s who recognised him as *their* leader did think his power was legitimate, they did see him as having authority.)

Why, then, do some people recognise that others have authority over them? Max Weber (1968), writing in the early twentieth century, made an influential distinction between different sources of authority. One source is tradition: it comes to be recognised that a certain way of doing things involving particular people making the decisions and exercising most of the power is the way things have always been done, and for no other reason this may be taken as the right way of doing things. Many people in the world have exercised power which others have recognised as legitimate simply on the basis of tradition.

But Weber pointed out that in the modern world, tradition has increasingly been questioned as a source of legitimacy. People want to know *why* they should do what someone else tells them to, and 'because this is the way it has always been done' is not an adequate answer. Instead, we have systems of rules (including the legal systems of states) which give positions of power to the people holding certain roles, occupancy of those roles is subject to some form of qualification and the whole system can be seen to be justified by broader considerations such as the general welfare. 'Bureaucracy' – as a sociological term, not necessarily pejorative – is the general term for systems of this sort, and the kind of authority involved is 'rational-legal'.

This is, of course, the kind of basis on which most leaders and managers within modern educational systems have their authority. As Hodgkinson says (1991: 54), 'modern state-financed education is essentially bureaucratic in its structure'. (See Hodgkinson (1978: ch. 5) and Peters (1966: ch. 9) for general treatments of the nature of power and authority and the relation between them.)

It is part of a system of rational-legal authority that it is not an arbitrary matter which people get into which positions. (We are talking here in terms of what Weber would call an *ideal type*; actual systems will not always work like this in practice.) The system makes the occupancy of positions of authority dependent on some sort of qualification. People normally have to apply for a position of authority, in competition with others, and show that they are qualified to do the job, either by virtue of their experience or (increasingly in modern systems) by having gained certain formal qualifications.

It follows that, if the system is working well, everyone who is in a position of authority will be qualified for that position. Nevertheless, it is still the case that the authority that someone has by virtue of their position within a bureaucratic system does not automatically go with the actual power to get things done. Occasionally someone may get into a position of authority who, despite formally being qualified for the job, actually has

little influence over others. And even among people who fill authority
roles reasonably well, some will be better leaders than others.

These points give us two important questions about individual positions
of authority in educational systems:

- First, what sort of knowledge, experience or formal qualifications should
  a system of educational authority seek in individuals who are going to
  fill positions of authority? The next section will take up some aspects of
  this question without attempting anything like a full answer.
- Second, among people who meet the formal requirements, what is it
  that makes some people better than others? Are there special sorts of
  personal qualities (over and above relevant experience and formal qualifications) which make for good leadership? After the next section, that
  will be the overarching topic of the rest of the chapter.

The authority of knowledge and expertise

While rational-legal systems of authority do indeed appear rational, this
does not mean that those selected as authorities can do their jobs simply
by following the rules of the system. You will probably be familiar with the
idea that any practical task, including both teaching and educational
administration, cannot be captured in a set of rules that can be codified
and taught. There is always an element needed of judgement in specific
circumstances. These are matters discussed, for instance, by Schön (1983)
in his well known work on the reflective practitioner, and by a number of
other writers in recent years who have drawn on the ancient Aristotelian
idea of *phronesis*, often translated as *practical wisdom* (cf. McLaughlin,
1999). The capacity to exercise sound practical judgement in specific circumstances is not the same thing as having a lot of theoretical knowledge,
but at the same time it does *depend* on having relevant theoretical knowledge. Think of a skilled doctor: she is able to see what is the best way to
respond to the specific condition of a specific patient at a specific time, but
she can only do this because she has acquired a great deal of knowledge
about healthy and diseased conditions.

The idea that people in positions of leadership should be people who
have the relevant knowledge is an idea that goes back at least to Plato. In
the present context, we can treat this idea of relevant knowledge as another kind of *authority*, one that was not treated by Weber as a distinct category but which has been brought out by some educational writers such as
Peters (1966: 239ff.). This is the kind of authority we refer to in academic
contexts, as when we say that writers such as Christopher Hodgkinson or
Peter Gronn (whom we shall encounter later in this chapter) are *authorities*
in the academic field of educational leadership. To call someone an authority in this sense is to say that on the basis of their research and learning

their views within a particular field ought to be taken seriously (which is not saying that they are necessarily correct in all their views).

It is important to notice that authority in this academic sense is relative, not absolute, in several ways:

- It is relative to a particular field of knowledge or experience, so the fact that someone is an authority in some area of science, for instance, does not by itself give any authority to that person's moral or political views. And the fact that someone is an authority in one of the subjects taught within a school or college does not by itself mean that this person knows better than others how to run a school or college.
- It is relative to the overall state of knowledge and experience in a given field at a given time. Newton and Einstein were both among the highest authorities in physics in their day, though Einstein's work undermined some of Newton's fundamental assumptions, and some of Einstein's own work is now increasingly being questioned. The knowledge of authorities is provisional and may be overturned.
- When experts take a teaching role, their authority is relative to the knowledge and experience of those they are teaching. Relative to the average university lecturer in physics, there may be only a few dozen people in the world who are authorities on black holes. But the average university teacher of physics is an authority in his or her field relative to the average undergraduate. And the average teacher of physics in a high school is an authority on physics relative to the average high school student. (It is compatible with this that a committed student may eventually come to know more than their teacher.)

You should keep these points about the relative nature of academic authority in mind as you think about the ideas in this book. As pointed out in the Introduction, I am drawing on the field called ethics or moral philosophy. Relative to most teachers, I could probably claim some authority in that field, but on the concrete context of running a school I can claim no authority. You may well know more about that than I do. That is one reason why, as I said at the beginning, the ideas in this book are ones for you to engage with in your own thinking, not ones to assimilate passively.

As you think about how you carry out your own leadership role, or will carry it out if you have that role in the future, consider what kinds of authority you have that are or will be relevant. In your teaching, you have some degree of authority in certain areas of knowledge relative to your students (whatever their age), and some knowledge (perhaps acquired mainly through experience) of how to teach your subject. Do these kinds of knowledge give you a basis for authority as a leader?

The answer is, probably not. It has often been assumed in practice that if someone is a good teacher then they will make a good administrator.

(Harber and Davies (1997: 6) refer to the prevalence of this assumption in developing countries.) But it is increasingly being recognised now that the knowledge and skills needed are different. This is at least part of the reason why many educational systems are developing programmes for the training and qualification of educational managers and leaders. (In the next chapter I shall refer to one such example, that produced in England by the National College for School Leadership.)

Make a list of the kinds of authority that you exercise (or will exercise) in your own leadership role. What is the scope of your authority, that is what restrictions are there on your authority to pursue your own sense of moral purpose? What are the sources of your authority?

If you gained your leadership position because you were recognised as a good teacher, this may be an element of traditional authority in action – this is the way it has generally been done. If you gained your leadership position because, even before you were in that formal position, people tended to look up to you and to take notice of your opinions, then it may be – though you are probably not the best person to claim this about yourself – that you have certain special personal qualities! (We'll come back to this later in this chapter.)

But whatever the route by which you got there, you are now in a position which, by virtue of its place within the system, gives you certain responsibilities and the powers to fulfil those responsibilities – this is an element of rational-legal authority. And if the system within which you hold that authority does not already demand a specific knowledge qualification, such demands will become increasingly likely in the future.

Charisma

As we noted above, even when someone has all the qualifications that the system demands from a leader, he or she may still turn out to be better or worse as a leader compared to someone else. This is the kind of point that seems evident from experience but which is quite difficult to study in a systematic way. Researchers have, however, tried to identify the personal qualities of a good leader. A number of writers on educational leadership have stressed the importance of the individual person as leader. For instance, Greenleaf (1996) wrote:

> In the end, it is the *person*, the leader as an individual, who counts. Systems, theories, organization structures are secondary. It is the inspiration and initiative of individual persons that move the world along. (Greenleaf, 1996: 334, quoted by Gronn, 2003: 262; italics in the original).

The mention of 'inspiration' calls to mind a third source of authority that Weber alluded to – *charisma*. The idea of *charisma* would be very hard to define in any way that could be used in empirical research. Writers mentioning charisma tend to refer to certain stock examples – such as Christ, Mohammed, Gandhi, Martin Luther King or Nelson Mandela – rather than offering definitions. Citing such examples, or speaking of 'sheer force of personal magnetism' (Bottery, 1992: 39) is to speak of something that could not be built into any system: no system of training or selection could guarantee that educational leaders were people with charisma.

It is not even clear that having educational leaders with personal charisma is an ideal. Charismatic people may be able too readily to get other people to follow them wherever they lead, and where they lead is not necessarily a good place to go. Hitler seems to have had charisma as a leader. And even if charisma could in some way be tamed, fitted into a bureaucratic system (which is perhaps a contradiction in terms), the charismatic leader cannot go on for ever. At some point, he or she has to have a successor, and if the successor lacks charisma the effective leadership may collapse.

Despite these problems, it seems that 'many commentators continue to hanker after great charismatic leadership' (Gronn, 2003: 269). The quotation is from an article in which Peter Gronn explores two ideas: the idea of individual greatness in a leader, and the idea that the good leader serves those whom he or she leads.

Gronn is sceptical about the idea that perceived greatness in a leader can be traced to personal charisma. There will often be situational factors that determine whether someone comes to be perceived this way. Citing Russel Ward (1990), he considers that the only determinant of 'greatness' is that someone has come to have a lasting reputation, and there may be various accidental reasons why that has happened in the case of one person and not in the case of another.

Leaders who have come to be perceived as great (including some who have actually come to be known as 'the Great', such as Alexander and Catherine) have not necessarily been ones who have brought much benefit to the people whom they have led or have dominated. The motivation of great leaders has sometimes been wealth, power, glory or self-aggrandisement. Yet the idea of service is not incompatible with greatness in reputation. Many political and religious leaders have claimed to serve their people or their followers; in some cases it may be that part of the reason why certain leaders have come to be seen as great is that their claim to be serving others is plausible (think again of Gandhi or Martin Luther King).

Gronn does not dismiss entirely the idea that there are particular qualities we should demand of our leaders. A disposition to serve others through leadership may itself be one of these qualities.

Characteristics of the good leader

Under this title, it would be convenient if we could simply list, on the basis
of experience and research, the personal qualities of a good leader. But the
task would not be a simple one because 'characteristics' or 'qualities' are
not all of a kind. In this section I shall have to distinguish at least three
value-related categories: the educational and ethical principles that leaders
pursue; their personal dispositions or 'virtues'; and what it is that fundamentally motivates them. In addition to these three categories, of course,
educational leaders need a whole range of practical competencies, including both technical skills and social interpersonal skills. I am not emphasising these practical competencies here, partly because many other people
have written about them, and more particularly because in themselves they
are ethically neutral. That means they can be used for good or bad ends.
Aristotle pointed out long ago that the knowledge and skills of a doctor can
be used to kill people as well as to cure them (a fact illustrated in Britain in
recent years in the case of the general practitioner Harold Shipman who was
found guilty of killing many elderly patients). Even interpersonal skills,
such as the ability to understand what someone else is thinking and feeling, can be used by one who is manipulating others into following her own
point of view as well as by one who wants others to share her values for
their own reasons. It is the fact that skills as such can be used for good or
bad that makes the question of motivation fundamental.

What are the characteristics of a good leader? Make a list of what you consider to
be the most important characteristics of a good leader in education.

To make this manageable, try to list at least four characteristics and not more
than eight. Then compare your list with those given below.

Here are six informal lists of the characteristics of a good leader, as identified by six students taking a course on educational leadership:

- respect, be fair-minded and have a sense of responsibility;
- confidence, courage, clarity of thought and purpose;
- vision, ability to motivate, team skills, delegation, analysis and reflection, listen, network and see the big picture;
- analytical, good interpersonal skills, integrity;
- respect for people, risk-taking and time in the classroom – focus on
  education;
- strategic thinking, empowerment of others, creating an open culture,
  attention to details.

The list in Table 3.1 is from research carried out by Kouzes and Posner
(1996), cited in Foreman (1998: 18–19).

Table 3.1 Characteristics of admired leaders

	1995 respondents: % of people selecting	1987 respondents: % of people selecting
Honest	88	83
Forward-looking	75	62
Inspiring	68	58
Competent	63	67
Fair-minded	49	40
Supportive	41	32
Broad-minded	40	37
Intelligent	40	43
Ambitious	13	21
Loyal	11	11
Self-controlled	5	13
Independent	5	10

Two more lists of characteristics found in successful principals can be taken from case-study research by Anne Gold and her colleagues in Britain. The principals they studied

> ... were concerned with such matters as inclusivity, equal opportunities and equity or justice, high expectations, engagement with stakeholders, co-operation, teamwork, commitment and understanding.
>
> The case studies provide insights into how some of these values and beliefs were demonstrated through the words and deeds of school leaders. Related to these strongly held values, and mentioned by case-study interviewees, were the personal qualities of school leaders. These included openness, accessibility, compassion, honesty, transparency, integrity, consistency, decisiveness, risk-taking, and an awareness of others and their situations. (Gold et al., 2003: 136)

Looking over these various lists as a whole, one point to be made about them is that the characteristics included are not all of a kind. Some seem to be intellectual abilities, some are the kinds of skills that it may be possible to learn, some may be a matter of personality, and some are more clearly ethical or moral. I shall concentrate on the latter in the rest of this chapter.

Principles in leadership

The philosophical study of ethics has in recent years divided into two broad strands (this itself is a broad simplification but adequate for the immediate purpose). One strand has been concerned with ethical principles: what should these be and how can they be justified? The other strand has been concerned with the qualities that make a person a good person: in a word (which used to be old-fashioned but is coming back into use) *virtues*.

Notice that in the quotation above Gold and her colleagues give two lists of values. In the first list – inclusivity, equal opportunities and equity or justice, high expectations, engagement with stakeholders, cooperation, teamwork, commitment and understanding – we can identify at least some of the items as *principles* that leaders can consciously follow. The second list, as Gold and her colleagues say, is a list of personal qualities: openness, accessibility, compassion, honesty, transparency, integrity, consistency, decisiveness, risk-taking and an awareness of others and their situations. These items could be considered as *virtues* of a leader.

Both of these lists could be said to identify *values* in a broad sense of that term, but it is worth noting some of the differences between considerations of principle, and virtues. In Chapter 1 we looked at important ethical principles, such as equality of opportunity, focusing on how they could be justified. Here, where we are concentrating on individual qualities, we need to ask about the motivation people may have for following principles.

It is an important feature of principles that they can be put into action without the person implementing them necessarily being driven by a particular kind of motivation. Principles, can, for instance, function even in a thoroughly bureaucratic situation. Suppose a government minister asks her civil servants to devise policies that will promote equal opportunities in schools. The minister might be motivated chiefly by the desire to win the next election and the civil servants may be simply doing their job without any personal commitment to the cause of equal opportunities. Nevertheless, if the civil servants do their job well they will devise policies that actually do something to promote equal opportunities. So the importance of broad ethical principles is not reducible to the motivation of individuals. Another illustration of this is that we can appeal to broad principles when we evaluate an institution or practice. We might say that a school is effective in meeting certain attainment targets but does not do as well as it should in terms of equal opportunities or inclusivity and is rather lacking in the transparency of its decision-making procedures. The reasons why this is so, and whether any criticism of the competence or motivation of individuals is merited, is a separate question.

It may be that when Hodgkinson, in the schema we looked at in Chapter 1, discusses what he calls transrational principles, he is not clearly distinguishing questions of what if anything might justify the principles from questions of what motivates a person to hold and follow certain principles. It may be a moot point whether any further reason can be given *why* a person *ought* to value justice or dignity. (Within certain religious perspectives, for instance, a further reason may be found in the nature of persons as being made in the image of God.) That is a question of the justification of the principles. Motivation is a different issue. Suppose we find that a school principal is determined that in her school all the students should be treated fairly. And suppose that, looking further into the principal's motivation, we find that the reason she is doing this is a worry that if any student is treated unfairly the parents will get to know about it and the school's reputation will suffer. Then we might say that this principal does not put a fundamental value on fairness for its own sake; or at least, while for her as a person fairness may be genuinely important, there is something else that as a principal she is even more concerned about. She is pursuing a policy of fairness as a means to an end, for the sake of the school's reputation.

It is perhaps implicit in Hodgkinson's discussion of principles at his Level 3 that the force of these principles for the persons who hold them is not *extrinsic* or *instrumental* but *intrinsic* – persons hold principles at this level if they value, say, fairness or dignity in their own right, not as means to something else. Someone who holds the principles in this way really *cares* about fairness or about dignity. To hold certain values at a fundamental level is not just to have certain thoughts or to accept a certain intellectual position; it involves feeling and commitment, not just thinking, however rational the thinking may be. Because of this, it does not follow from the possibility of giving a rational justification for a principle that anyone will actually be motivated to follow the principle. That is why, if we want not just to consider which values should be important in education, but also to think about how these values can be built into the practice of education, we have to consider questions of motivation. The motivation that is appropriate for a civil servant designing policies to implement equal opportunities may be different from the motivation that is desirable for the school head trying to realise equal opportunities in her school.

Virtues in leadership

How a person is motivated ties in with the broader question of what sort of person she is. This brings us to the category of *virtues*. A *virtue* (in the sense of the term that is now common in philosophical discussion of ethics and which is often traced back to Aristotle) is a desirable personal quality of a complex sort, combining cognitive awareness, affective response and motivation to act. To illustrate this it will be best to take a quality that would be very widely recognised as a virtue, and which also appears in the list of personal qualities cited above from Gold et al.: compassion.

Following the clue above, that a virtue combines cognitive awareness, affective response and motivation to act, can you express in your own words the qualities a person has if he or she is compassionate?

To be a compassionate person is, among other things, to be liable to notice when someone else is troubled or suffering. Someone who lacks compassion may not even notice that someone else is suffering (it is not obvious what the appropriate word is for this condition: perhaps callousness). But this perceptual, cognitive ability and tendency to be aware of another's state is not enough by itself to make a person compassionate. A sadist has the ability and tendency to notice when someone else is in pain, but the sadist derives pleasure from this.

The second aspect of a virtue, then, is an affective one. The compassionate person has empathy, is moved negatively in her own feelings – not positively, like the sadist – by her awareness of the other's pain. But then we have to add, thirdly, that this will not be just a passive feeling; the compassionate person will be motivated to do something to help the other. The compassionate person is not, of course, actively helping others at every moment. But she tends to be motivated in such a way that she actually does help when it is appropriate to do so.

The last point illustrates the fact that a virtue is a tendency or *disposition* to respond to situations in appropriate ways. Aristotle, and many other commentators, would say that the tendency, if it really is to be counted a virtue, has to exist to the right degree – not too much, not too little. The virtue of courage, for instance, involves recognising danger and having the willingness to face up to it to the degree appropriate to the circumstances – not the cowardice of always retreating from danger, but also not the recklessness of caring nothing about it at all.

Not every personal quality that we find desirable or admirable in a person will necessarily fit this model of what a virtue is. In different cases the cognitive aspect, or the affective aspect, or the motivational aspect, may be less clear. And it is debatable whether the idea that a virtue falls in the mean between extremes applies to all cases. Nevertheless, if we want to take our thinking about the personal qualities of a leader beyond a simple list of names, it will be helpful to think about how far the various qualities we might name do fit this pattern. For instance, what about the items in the list of personal qualities cited from Gold et al.?

Look again at the items in the list of personal qualities cited from Gold et al.: openness, accessibility, compassion, honesty, transparency, integrity, consistency, decisiveness, risk-taking and an awareness of others and their situations. Do all of these qualities count as virtues in the sense described above? Do they all have perceptual/cognitive, affective and motivational elements? Is the desirable quality, in every case, somewhere between a corresponding deficiency and an excess?

We have just seen that compassion fits, as it were, the full model of what a virtue is. Some of the other items on the list do not seem to involve the same cognitive and affective elements: risk-taking, for instance. But notice that the willingness to take risks is a quality, like courage, that one person might have to too great an extent, while another person might have it to an insufficient extent.

If you have grasped the distinction between principles and virtues, you could consider whether using this distinction will be helpful to you in a leadership role. Remember that we can refer to principles and to personal qualities both in trying to decide what to do and in evaluating the actions of others. For ourselves, we can try to follow certain principles. Are we more likely to refer to personal qualities when we are thinking about the desirable characteristics of leadership not in ourselves, but in others?

Do you find it helpful to think in terms of virtues when you are reflecting on your own activity as a leader?

Even if we concentrate on virtues, you have seen that the qualities that people pick out as desirable in educational leaders are quite varied. Is there any rationale that could lead us to agree on a list?

The idea that certain roles demand certain virtues to a special degree is not unfamiliar. For instance, we may associate the virtue of compassion or caring with nurses, or the virtue of a sense of justice with judges, or the virtue of courage with soldiers. These virtues are the particular qualities needed by persons in these roles if they are to be able to fulfil those roles well. What about the role of educational leadership?

Look back at the list you made of what you consider to be the most important characteristics of a good leader in education. Concentrate now on the items in your list that seem to be personal qualities or virtues. Do you find that some of them would be desirable qualities in anyone while others may be especially desirable in educational leaders? How can we decide whether certain qualities are especially important for educational leaders?

One way of approaching this question would be to break it down into two smaller questions. Are there virtues especially needed by an educator as such? And are there virtues especially needed by a leader as such? Perhaps if we can find virtues special to each of these categories then we might find in the overlap between the two the virtues special to educational leadership. This seems to be an approach worth trying out.

Virtues in education and in leadership

The philosopher Alasdair MacIntyre (1992) has an influential argument that relates virtues to practices: roughly, virtues are the qualities necessary to the successful pursuit of a human practice. Jasper Ungoed-Thomas (1996: 150–2) has an argument influenced by MacIntyre to identify the virtues especially important in education. Treating education as a practice, he says that it must have certain central concerns: concerns with persons, with the curriculum, with community and with citizenship. He then identifies the 'first virtue' corresponding to each of these concerns: *respect* in relation to persons, *truth* in relation to curriculum, *fairness* in relation to community and *responsibility* in relation to citizenship. He concludes:

> Respect for persons, truth, fairness and responsibility are then the educationally necessary first virtues. (p. 153)

Whether or not you are persuaded by Ungoed-Thomas's argument, it would be hard to dispute that these *are* important qualities in education, perhaps alongside others. (Ungoed-Thomas goes on to mention cooperation, discipline, tolerance, hard work, compassion and honesty.) Since they are important in education, they must be important concerns for educational leaders as well as for other teachers. But this does not by itself show that any of these qualities picks out something that might be special about a *leader* in the field.

To come from a different angle, are there virtues that are especially important in *leaders* generally? The *idea* that there are certain personal qualities common to leaders is not an unusual one, but attempts to verify this idea by empirical studies – to identify a particular set of qualities that are clearly present in a range of leaders and transferable across cultures – have not been very successful. Our thinking about the qualities of leaders may partly rest on unwarranted and stereotypical assumptions. For instance, if people are asked about the qualities of male leaders and of female leaders their answers tend to reflect more general stereotypes about male and female qualities.

Of the personal qualities that Gold and her colleagues found in their study – openness, accessibility, compassion, honesty, transparency, integrity, consistency, decisiveness, risk-taking and an awareness of others and their situations – most seem to be good qualities for anyone to possess. But are some of them perhaps especially important for leaders? One that might seem to be is decisiveness – the idea of leadership seems to go with the willingness to come to decisions and stick to them. At least, this may be true for the kind of leadership that expects others to follow. When we look later at leadership in democratic contexts, where at least some decisions will be arrived at collectively, even the virtue of decisiveness may turn out to be more complex than it looks at first sight.

Another item in the list raises further interesting questions: risk-taking. Is risk-taking especially a quality we would associate with leaders? Risk-taking can certainly be more problematic for a leader than for someone whose decisions affect only themselves, since when the leader takes risks the consequences of getting something wrong will affect many other people as well. Realising that may lead some leaders or potential leaders to be overcautious. And to be overcautious is, of course, not a virtue in leaders since changes do often have to be made. So in a sense leaders do have to be willing to take risks, but what goes along with risk-taking, though not explicitly mentioned in the list above, is an acceptance of responsibility for the consequences of one's decisions.

It is not difficult to see the acceptance of responsibility going with the disposition to serve that Gronn focused on, as we saw above. The disposition to serve does do at least something to distinguish the educational leader from some other leaders. Some leaders, including some characteristically charismatic leaders in the past, may be concerned above all with their own advancement, power and glorification. But this could not (if Gronn is right) be the major motivation of a great educational leader. A commitment to the idea of education and the values that go with it is necessarily a commitment to the good of others. Whatever the psychological roots of the motivation may be, the direction of the commitment has to be altruistic and it has to be strong enough to carry through into practical consequences.

It may be that the need for the right kind of motivation, and a motivation that is strong enough, is the reason why we have to consider the personal qualities of educational leaders as well as their principles. As we saw above, a civil servant designing policies for equal opportunities and a headteacher putting such policies into practice may both be following the same principles, but they need a different quality of motivation. The civil servant may be simply doing her job and still design good policies. But a headteacher who is just 'doing her job' is less likely to be able to make the policies work in practice.

The headteacher needs virtues that the civil servant does not.

Summary

In this chapter we have considered the qualities or characteristics that may be required for an individual in a leadership role. First we looked at authority, and saw that within a bureaucratic system there will be certain formal qualifications for the holding of authority. This contrasts with the idea of a personal authority that comes from charisma. While charisma may be desirable, it cannot be required. But we can enquire into the desirable qualities in a leader. This was the theme of the rest of the chapter.

Here we distinguished the following of principles from the possession of virtues. We found a variety of ideas about the virtues of a good leader, but we did not find a definitive list or a conclusive way of identifying such qualities. The discussion suggests that, partly because of the difficulty of clearly identifying any list of the qualities of the good leader, we should not put too much reliance on the hope that the role of leadership can always be conducted by the 'right kind of individual'. We need to see how the qualities of individuals can function within a situation in which many factors cannot be directly under the control of a single individual. In later chapters we will take a more situational view of how leadership functions.

The next chapter will form a bridge between individual and situational concerns, by looking at the idea of vision.

Suggested further reading

Bottery, M. (1992) *The Ethics of Educational Management*. London: Cassell. See especially Chapter 12, 'The ethics of leadership', which starts from the individual model of leadership and moves towards a more situational approach, touching on many of the themes of this chapter.

Hodgkinson, C. (1999) 'Triumph of the will', in Begley, P. and Leonard, P. (eds), *The Values of Educational Administration*. London: Falmer. An example of Hodgkinson's writing in which he puts great weight on the qualities of the individual leader.

MacIntyre, A. (1992) *After Virtue*. London: Duckworth, Chapter 14. A philosophical discussion that has been very influential in directing attention towards virtues rather than the following of rules and principles.

Strike, K., Haller, E. and Soltis, J. (1998) *The Ethics of School Administration*, 2nd edn. New York: Teachers College Press, Chapter 6 'Educational authority'. I take a case study from this in Chapter 6 on community and democracy, but it is also relevant here for the questions it raises about who should have the authority to make educational decisions.

4 | Vision in education

This chapter will look in some depth at the idea of *vision*, which has become prominent in the discourse of educational leadership in recent years. What is vision in the context of education? *Whose* vision are we talking about? How does vision make a difference in education?

This chapter will help you to:

- understand what is meant by 'vision' in educational contexts;
- understand why vision is widely considered to be important in educational leadership;
- understand that the notion of vision might be misunderstood or misapplied;
- understand that in the view of most commentators it is important for vision to be shared within a school.

This chapter has four major sections: interpreting 'vision'; challenges to the idea of vision; the importance of shared vision; and an alternative vision. The section on challenges to the idea of vision is subdivided into three issues: the scope for individual vision within a wider educational contest; the 'fuzziness' of the idea of vision; and the danger of an individual vision being imposed on others. The final section presents as an example the way that a vision for schooling is worked out by one writer.

Suppose you are applying for a leadership position in education at a higher level than your present one and you are asked to describe your vision for education. What would you say?

Your response to this question will probably depend in part on whether you are already familiar with the idea that educational leaders need vision. Perhaps you were yourself asked about your vision at your last job interview. So you may have an answer ready to hand.

If the idea that an educational leader needs vision (or a vision) is not yet one you are accustomed to working with, this chapter will allow you to look into the possible merits and demerits of the idea.

Interpreting 'vision'

Perhaps the commonest use of the word 'vision' in English is to refer to the ordinary capacity for seeing; for instance, like many people, I wear glasses to correct a deficiency in my vision. Since vision in this everyday, literal, sense is a normal capacity of human beings it is not likely to be very helpful to a consideration of any special qualities needed in leadership.

It is possible to refine this ordinary notion of vision into something more special by making it metaphorical. Then, when we say that a person 'has vision', we mean that he or she has, not just the ordinary capacity of sight, but the ability, to a greater extent than most, to see how things could be. We might call this quality 'imaginative perception' (I borrow the term from an unpublished doctoral thesis on school leadership by Janet Orchard). In the context of schools, it could be the capacity to see the possibilities that are open in the future of a school, perhaps to see possibilities that others might overlook, and to see how the school might get from where it is to a desirable future. A head with this capacity might be described as visionary.

We can talk, then, of vision as a capacity, a kind of metaphorical perception, but we can also talk of 'a vision' as an object, something that is perceived. This use of the word probably has its roots in the religious or mystical use in which a vision is something that appears to a person, as in the biblical prophecy 'Your old men shall dream dreams and your young men shall see visions' (Joel 2.28). When someone has a vision in this sense we may say that from the point of view of the ordinary everyday world the appearance is not real, yet it can seem to the person who experiences it to have more reality or truth then everyday experience. Such a vision, then, can inspire the person who has it to greater effort, or at least to hope rather than despair.

When the notion of vision is used in contexts of educational leadership it often has connotations both of the capacity to see something beyond what is immediately present – the current status quo – and of that which is seen – a representation of the future. When we speak of a person's vision for her school, we are speaking of her picture of what it could be or will be like in the future. But to put it that way is to make it seem rather mundane. Anyone could have a mental picture of what a school will be like in future, but in many cases the picture might not be of a kind that would motivate or inspire people. If we use the term 'vision' for just any picture of what a school will be like, we will be losing the sense that there is something special about a vision.

As Ungoed-Thomas puts it, vision 'needs to be interpreted as a high word. As such, it can offer an ideal of what a school should be. It should help to give schools a continuing, secure and permanent sense of what they ought to be doing' (Ungoed-Thomas, 1996: 146).

How does vision differ from moral purpose?

In Chapter 2 we looked at the idea of purpose, including the moral purpose that can motivate a leader. In educational contexts 'vision', like 'purpose', denotes that something is being aimed at. And also, like purpose, vision can give a sense of direction and of motivation. But vision differs from purpose in that it presents a picture of how things will be at some point in the future, which purpose does not necessarily do. A sense of purpose might be focused on something relatively narrow, such as improving test scores or improving recruitment to the school. Or a sense of purpose might be broader but quite ill-defined – if, for instance, a head wanted to keep her school improving, but had no very clear idea of what the school would be like after a period of improvement. Or a leader's purpose could even be to keep things much the same as they are, if the leader considers that the way things are is already quite good. But to have this sort of purpose is clearly not to be driven by a vision of how things might be.

In practice it may not be easy to say whether someone is not just pursuing a valuable purpose but is driven by a vision. Consider one of the principals mentioned by Michael Fullan in the discussion of moral purpose to which I referred in Chapter 2:

> Dr Newman knew that he needed to establish trusting relationships with all members of his school community to advance its improvement efforts. He was articulate about what this meant to him. 'Trust is built by contact, by consistency, by doing what you say you're going to do, by showing concern, by acting on solutions, [but] mostly by doing what you say you're going to do.' Throughout our interviews, Dr Newman talked at length about the importance of positive social relations in the functioning of a good school, and felt strongly that developing trust was critical within his school community. (From Bryk and Schneider, 2002: 38–9, quoted in Fullan, 2003: 32).

We could clearly say that Dr Newman has a moral purpose, which is about establishing trusting relationships. (And, of course, it may also be about all sorts of other educational purposes that are not mentioned in this passage.) And he clearly has improvement in mind. But there is no sense (at least within this quotation) of a goal towards which the improvement is heading. There is no rich picture of what the school should be like, beyond the fact that people within it will have trusting relationships with each other. There does not seem to be enough depth or detail in this idea for us to describe it as a vision of how things will be.

For an idea such as 'vision' we should not expect a precise or stable definition. You will probably find that you encounter many slightly different definitions in the work that you read. Here is one that encapsulates many of the aspects to which writers often refer:

Vision An image of what might be; an ideal which is unique to the person or the organisation and recognises dissatisfaction with the present. It is a catalyst for action, and reflects core values: 'A vision is a preferred future, a desirable state. It is an expression of optimism despite the bureaucratic surroundings or evidence to the contrary'. (Block, 1987: 103, quoted in Foreman, 1998: 22).

Vision as personal

In Ungoed-Thomas's view, vision is essentially personal:

Of its nature, it appears to individuals ... That visions are seen properly by individuals has significant implications. It is identifiable human beings, not the spokepersons of associations, who observe, explain, communicate, inspire, can be questioned, who are answerable. Vision described by an institution is anonymous in origin, at best a mirage designed to offer comfort, at worst a device intended to promote hierarchical control. (Ungoed-Thomas, 1996: 147)

Ungoed-Thomas is not the only commentator to have thought of educational vision as essentially individual. Orchard (2004), writing particularly in the British context, points out that many advertisements for headteachers specify that the applicant must have vision, and that some headteachers themselves see what they are doing in terms of putting their vision into effect. She quotes John Dunford, General Secretary of the Secondary Headteachers Association (in England):

The reason I enjoyed the job [of headteacher] so much had nothing to do with achieving targets or implementing the National Curriculum or getting a good inspection report or surviving another interminable governor's meeting, but because I could dream dreams and then go into school the next morning and put them into action. In other words, headship is about creativity and vision and leadership.

It is at this point that we need to be careful in interpreting just *how* headteachers may, and should, put their dreams into action. *Should* leadership be about one person putting his or her dreams into action?
   Bottery quotes Simon as saying:

... dreams are never neutral; they are always SOMEONE's dreams, and to the degree that they are implicated in organizing the future for others, they always have a moral and political dimension. (Bottery, 1992: 185)

Think, then, of a leader relatively unconstrained by bureaucratic rules and regulations, who has a dream that others are inspired to follow. Perhaps Martin Luther King's 'I have a dream' speech will come to mind. King is a prime example of a person with a reputation for a certain personal magnetism or *charisma* – an idea you encountered in the previous chapter. What is important for the moment is that the charismatic leader is someone who attracts followers, and that the followers may to some degree give up their own judgement as they follow their leader's dream.

Here we need to ask whether there is a danger in the idea that educational leadership should consist in one person having a dream that others follow. Other commentators have raised this point. Bottery goes on to say:

> Visionaries all too easily become charismatic, then fascist and authoritarian, as they prosecute their personal conceptions. (Bottery, 1992: 185)

Foreman cites Starratt, who suggested that some earlier writers would have rejected the term 'vision' as being:

> ... too fuzzy, too unquantifiable, too impossible to operationalize in one or two variables. It smacks of religious fervour. It is something one would associate with that other psychiatrically suspect category, 'charisma'. (Starratt, 1993: 7, quoted in Foreman, 1998: 20–1)

Foreman also cites Stacey on the dangers of vision, including the fact that:

> Vision-building places heavy burdens on leaders and may lead to follower dependency or groupthink and the perpetuation of the belief that the success of organisation relies on one or two gifted individuals. (Adapted from Stacey, 1992: 137–40 and quoted in Foreman, 1998: 21)

Such quotations raise criticisms about the idea of vision that need to be taken seriously. In what follows we can address three points:

- How much room is there, in contemporary educational systems, for a leader to have an individual vision?
- Is it correct that, in Starratt's words, vision is 'too fuzzy, too unquantifiable, too impossible to operationalize'?
- How serious is the danger that a leader's personal vision will be imposed on followers?

Challenges to the idea of vision

Individual leadership within a wider vision

We shall approach the first question through an example taken from Malaysia.

Vision 2020 in Malaysia

Molly Lee (1999) has reported on the educational policies being pursued by the Malaysian government within the context of broader social goals:

> In January 1991, the Malaysian government unveiled its Vision 2020, the year by which Malaysia would achieve the status of an industrialized and developed country in terms of it economy, national unity, social cohesion, social justice, political stability, system of government, quality of life social and spiritual values, national pride and confidence ... Education is to play an important role in helping the country to meet the above challenges. (Lee, 1999: 87)

Lee goes on to detail the various ways in which the country looked to education to help it achieve the ambitious goals of Vision 2020. For our purposes here, the central question concerns how much scope there could be for leaders within education to develop any vision of their own, when the government has already outlined so much of the wider vision to which education is expected to contribute.

In fact, Vision 2020, even while it gave central expression to its overall goals, believed that decentralisation within the education system was an important means towards those goals:

> Decentralisation implies devolution of decision-making, empowerment and enablement. Decentralisation of educational management can only be effective if schools are managed by personnel who have a high sense of professionalism. Effective school leadership is essential for school-based management. School heads are required to provide not only administrative leadership but also instructional leadership ...
>
> ... If decision-making were to be devolved from top to bottom then personnel at the centre should learn how to 'let go' whereas those at the periphery must learn how to 'take up' the responsibilities. But before school heads or teachers are able to 'take up' these responsibilities, they must be equipped professionally.
>
> ... Good school-based management requires effective school leadership whereby school heads are able to handle both internal school operation as well as the school–environment interaction. (Lee, 1999: 92–3)

We noted at the end of Chapter 2 that educational leadership always functions within some wider set of public expectations and political goals relating to the purposes of education. In contemporary discourse a government's plans for education may themselves be framed in the terminology of 'vision'. The Malaysian case is one example of this. We shall consider another example of this below when we look at the work of the National College for School Leadership in England.

This picture outlined in Malaysia would fit many countries, though with variations. There will normally be a policy at government level incorporating its own goals for education, and school leaders will be expected to work within this. But, in line with Molly Lee's comments, we must expect leaders to be responsible professionals who have the capacity to work within government policy without slavishly following it. Leaders have to make decisions in the light of the conditions applying at particular times and places and these conditions can never be anticipated in detail at the level of policy. When leaders decide how best to put a policy into effect in their particular circumstances, they are inevitably using their professional judgement in interpreting the policy. Any policy that allows space for leadership at all must, then, allow some space for interpretation.

It is in this way that the idea of vision at the level of a school is appropriate. Government will expect school leaders to share the overall purposes for education that the government sets, but within overall government policy there can be room for leaders to formulate their own visions for their own schools, and to pursue this vision with the sense of moral purpose that Fullan speaks of. Just how much room there is for individual vision can vary widely from one educational system to another.

At one end of the scale are systems that are highly bureaucratic. In the case of Malaysia, Lee reports that 'there is a move towards decentralisation from a highly centralised and bureaucratic system'. But it is clear from her report that this decentralisation consists partly in the establishment of offices at district level. The role of the officers at district level is 'to ensure that educational policies made at the centre are carried out at the school level and that complaints and needs at the school level are communicated to the centre.' There appears to be still a degree of bureaucratic control here at a level above the school.

Articulating leadership values in England

The school system in England is one in which there is strong emphasis on schools meeting targets that are set by central government. This has led one commentator, as we saw in Chapter 2, to refer to the system as one encouraging only 'bastard leadership'. But Gold and her colleagues found that the heads they studied were:

> ... principled individuals with a strong commitment to their 'mission', determined to do the best for their schools, particularly for the pupils and students within them. They endeavoured to mediate the many externally driven directives to ensure, as far as it was possible, that their take-up was consistent with what the school was trying to achieve. (Gold et al., 2003: 136)

Reporting on a later piece of research Gold says:

> Overall, the school leaders articulated a strongly held set of developmental and educational values which they believed informed their leadership

approach to working with students. While the UK government's emphasis on standards, particularly attainment and behaviour, had some resonance with the school leaders' values, these were articulated broadly and in combination with a wider set of developmental and educational values. (Gold, 2004: 17)

The research of Gold and her colleagues, then, suggests that in England there is real scope for heads to pursue a particular vision for their school.

How to work within the bureaucracy

Pursuing a vision for one school within a bureaucratic system brings its own difficulties. Here is one writer's view from the United States. Thomas Sergiovanni (2005) agrees about the importance of vision, and agrees about the bureaucratic constraints under which many schools operate:

> Papers must be filed, data must be accumulated, teachers must be evaluated according to rules, schedules must be followed, and so on ... (Sergiovanni, 2005: 17)

Within this system, the possibilities for a school leader look pretty bleak:

> If local school leaders follow these rules to the letter, excellence remains out of reach and basic competence is endangered. If they do not follow these rules, they might find themselves in trouble ... (Sergiovanni, 2005: 17)

What is the solution? What Sergiovanni calls 'building in canvas' – 'like the folding canvas tanks the US military built to serve as decoys while creating an illusion of strength'. Sergiovanni spells out what this means in the following paragraph:

> Schools have multiple and often conflicting purposes that make exact alignment of structure and purpose difficult, if not impossible. In the real world schools must look the way they are supposed to. To obtain legitimacy the school must be able to communicate to its sponsors [Sergiovanni means the bureaucrats who control authorisation and funding] a feeling of competence. In return it receives needed statements of confidence. Because of their relative remoteness, bureaucratic sponsors are attracted to the general features of school structure rather than to the details of how these features are being interpreted in day-to-day schooling. Therefore, schools have a surprising amount of freedom as they interpret policies and rules in ways that support sensible teaching and learning. (Sergiovanni, 2005: 17)

Sergiovanni goes further than most writers in advocating 'working the system' for educational ends: in effect, creating the illusion that all the demands of the system are being met, so as to gain the freedom to do what seems to the leader to be the right thing to do. He acknowledges that some people might find this procedure morally questionable, but suggests that what is more morally questionable is trying to ignore realities so as to 'push ill-fitting management theories'.

How far do you think it is alright for school leaders to create the illusion that all the external demands are being met in order to satisfy external authorities if they are doing this for the sake of concentrating on what is really important?

Bottery has also raised this issue: see Bottery (2004: 89–94). He reports:

> There is evidence that, under current target-driven regimes, some individuals do manage to work the system successfully, as they knowingly 'play the game' while at the same time keeping their eye on 'the real' issues, needs and desired developments of their organizations.

But Bottery goes on to report that many teachers (not only those in leadership roles) find that knowingly 'playing the game' makes them lose their self-respect and feel demoralised. In evidence he cites Day et al. (2000), Jeffrey and Woods (1998) and Hargreaves (2003).

To summarise on our first question above – how much room is there, in contemporary educational systems, for a leader to have an individual vision? – the examples from Malaysia, England and America suggest that there can be quite a lot of room, but that there may be a personal cost in pursuing this individual vision.

Is vision too 'fuzzy'?

Our second question about vision was: is vision 'too fuzzy, too unquantifiable, too impossible to operationalize?'

This question is important not only for researchers. Increasingly it may come to be a firm expectation on heads and principals that they have what is called a vision for their school. It may come to be that an applicant for a leadership post will have to persuade an appointing committee that he or she does have such a vision. But how can this be established? Will it be entirely down to the impressions of an appointing committee to say whether an applicant has a vision for the school they wish to lead?

In an article called 'The concept of vision in educational effectiveness theory and research', Bert Creemers and Gerry Reezigt (1999) try to 'operationalise' the concept of vision. Creemers and Reezigt write not only about vision but also about a variety of what they call 'vision-related concepts'. At a national level, these are concepts of educational goals, standards and values; at a school level, concepts of educational leadership, school mission and school climate; at the classroom level, concepts of teachers' beliefs about education, teachers' expectations and 'teacher efficacy'. Linking vision to all of these concepts enables the authors to tap into a considerable amount of empirical research tending to show the importance of these different variables. They seem to treat 'vision' as something of a compendium term, taking in all of these different factors. But that does not mean that the notion of vision itself has become something measurable.

Creemers and Reezigt's desire to see vision as something that can be tied down, made concrete, perhaps influences their definition of vision:

> A fully elaborated vision on education links educational goals and educational means in an instrumental way. Although focusing on the educational dimension, it also specifies the role and meaning of pedagogical, psychological and sociological notions about education. (Creemers and Reezigt, 1999: 128)

One way in which this definition of vision differs from many is that Creemers and Reezigt think there is an instrumental component to vision: in other words, it concerns means and not just ends. For many writers, including Block, a vision is a picture of a desired state. Of course, no one would dispute that a leader must not just have a desirable end in mind, but also needs to find means for getting there. The dispute is only over whether the means count as part of the vision. This may sound like a dispute over a word, but it may be important if we are considering whether the idea of vision can be operationalised. This is because it will always be easier for researchers to make comparisons between the means used by different leaders – looking, for instance, at the procedures and structures that leaders establish within their schools – and to establish correlations between procedures and measures of a school's success than to establish any direct effect of a leader having or not having an image of a desired future in mind, or having one sort of image rather than another.

We asked whether the idea of vision is too fuzzy. Perhaps the answer is that it depends how we want to use the notion. Ungoed-Thomas wants it to be a 'high word'; Creemers and Reezigt want to operationalise it. But if the notion is operationalised, it will lose its highness, in other words it will lose the connotations that led to the use of the word vision in the first place. If vision is to be a high word, it is surely bound to have a certain fuzziness about it. That is not necessarily a matter for regret. As Aristotle pointed out long ago (*Nicomachean Ethics*, Book 1), in matters of values we should not expect the precision that we would expect in the sciences. If it is helpful at all to use the notion of vision to indicate a picture of what a school could be like, any such picture will inevitable be value-laden. To try to operationalise it may be to miss the point of the notion. But that does not settle the question of whether it is, all things considered, a helpful notion in education at all.

Imposing a personal vision?

Our third question above was: how serious is the danger that a leader's personal vision will be imposed on followers? In a sense this question is the opposite to the first: if a wider governmental vision does leave some room for an individual to pursue his or her own vision, is there a danger that it leaves *too much* room?

The National College for School Leadership in England

The National College for School Leadership (NCSL) 'provides learning and development opportunities and professional and practical support for school leaders at every stage in their career. [Its] core purpose is to develop individuals and teams to lead and manage their own schools and work collaboratively with others' (from www.ncsl.org.uk). Among other activities it produces learning materials for the National Professional Qualification for Headship. The idea of vision is prominent in these. One unit, 'Developing a strategic educational vision', is about how headteachers can develop their vision for their school, though it is clear that this is to be done within the government's vision for education in England. The next unit is about 'Securing the commitment of others to the vision'. This includes sections on 'The role of the headteacher in securing the commitment of others' and 'Selling the vision'.

This kind of language has led to some criticism. If the intention is that the government's vision for education should be promoted through training headteachers to develop their own vision for their school, which they then have to sell to their school, is the whole process a case of bureaucratic manipulation, in which headteachers have to manipulate their teachers into following what are ultimately the government's own aims? This is a gist of a critique we shall look at now (it is worth saying in advance that this critique may itself be open to criticism).

A critique of NCSL

Michael Smith (2002), a philosopher of education, in a detailed critique of the initiatives of the National College for School Leadership in England in effect argues that such imposition can happen even *within* a bureaucratic structure. Ostensibly, he claims, such an initiative is trying to get away from earlier bureaucratic conceptions:

> The previous mechanistic, systems-oriented conception has been set aside. The new emphasis is on creating aims, and developing an awareness of the way in which the school should evolve. Furthermore, this conception appears to give weight to a voluntaristic notion of the teacher as somebody who can be aware of and reflective about the assumed need for change; someone to whom the head can communicate her vision of the future. (Smith, 2002: 27)

But Smith goes on to make two main criticisms of this picture. First (and still in line with the danger of imposition mentioned above):

> It is the headteacher's vision of the school's goals which prevails. There is no talk of interaction here, no formulating of the school's aims together. On the other hand there is a requirement on the head to bring her staff to grasp the 'need' for change and, indeed, for them to understand the direction in which they must go. (Smith, 2002: 27)

So the head's role, Smith argues, is inevitably manipulative:

> … if she is to 'create a vision' and to establish unifying aims to achieve it she must engage in a detailed process of management, to plan long term, and, in so doing, not only to restrict any pluralistic aims the institution might have but, more importantly, constrain the professional autonomy of those acting within it … The other persons involved therefore are never acting for themselves, for their own ends, but always for somebody else's ends. (Smith, 2002: 34)

Bottery has made a similar point:

> … management as the use of different forms of power conceptualizes relationships within the school in a manipulative, means-to-end manner. People are not seen or valued as ends in themselves, but are being used, through the varieties of power available, to achieve other ends. (Bottery, 1992: 186)

So far, these points could equally be true of the charismatic leader who is getting others to follow her for her own ends. But, recognising that the head must herself be working within a broader administrative structure, Smith goes on to argue that the whole process is in a profound sense bureaucratic:

> The problem at the heart of this theory is that in preconceiving the aims of the institution, or in applying herself to carry out others' preconceived aims, the head is left with no other authority save that of Weber's bureaucratic manager [see the discussion of authority in the previous chapter]. For her primary concern is *not* to offer rational or ethical justifications in an attempt to bring her subordinates, through unity of purpose, to fulfil her aims … (Smith, 2002: 35)

So, in terms of the distinction between power and authority that we drew in Chapter 3, this head is 'the wielder of "successful power" as opposed to manifesting a justifiable and justifying authority'. Smith goes on to point out that even this power will not necessarily be wielded in a consistent direction, because what the head is aiming at, the direction in which she is trying to take the school, will itself be liable to vary according to the demands of government or the expectations of 'consumers'. 'The

management of change is therefore not grounded in moral principles ...'
(Smith, 2002: 35).

If Smith's criticisms are sound, then much of what is currently happening in school leadership is, as the title of his article suggests, 'ethically flawed'. But are the criticisms sound?

Taking into account your own experience both as teacher subject to the leadership of others and as leader yourself, consider whether the process by which a school leader gets others to share his or her vision is likely to be manipulative.

Smith writes on the basis of his analysis of literature from the School Leadership Initiative in England, bringing to bear on that his knowledge of a largely philosophical literature about ethics.

Smith's article was published in 2002. In the field of training for leadership, changes can happen quickly. For instance, the National Professional Qualification for Headship now works to a new set of National Standards for Headteachers, published in 2004 (which can be downloaded at http://publications.teachernet.gov.uk). These do use the language of 'shared' and 'collaborative' vision (especially in the section 'Shaping the future'). But the language of official documentation can only take us so far; other kinds of evidence – including the experience of those who have gained the National Professional Qualification – would be needed for a full assessment of the claim that there is something manipulative about the way that headteachers in England are expected to bring about the sharing of a vision in their schools.

Researchers who have directly observed what is happening in schools often take a more positive view of the importance of a leader's vision. For instance, Gold et al. (2003), referring partly to the same literature about the School Leadership Initiative, note that:

> Successful school leaders are driven by personal, moral and educational values and are able to articulate these with total conviction, creating a clear sense of institutional purpose and direction. (Gold et al., 2003: 135)

The importance of shared vision

It is clear from the article by Gold and her collaborators that they do not see the leader's exercise of values and vision as manipulative. On the contrary, they are concerned with 'the extent to which vision and values were shared and articulated by all who were involved in them' (Gold et al., 2003: 131). This theme, that a school's vision needs to be a shared vision, comes through in a great deal of the literature about vision. Another example comes from Sergiovanni:

Jackson-Keller School

I remember walking through the Jackson-Keller School in 1988 and was struck by the warmth and friendly interpersonal climate that I found everywhere. When Jackson-Keller reopened, the new principal, Alicia Thomas, had a vision: to create a school that would be a caring place for students. And she carefully selected a faculty that would fit the bill. Her strengths, as a leader, were focused on encouraging, motivating and building up the faculty and she did this by caring for them.

The teachers responded to her leadership with loyalty and appreciation and worked hard to be good and caring teachers. Jackson-Keller was a good school. Still, something was missing. Despite the magic of warmth, this faculty had much more of its talents to develop, to give, and to share.

Like a giant awakening from a slumber, there was a reawakening within this faculty as members began to push the principal and themselves for more. Though at first Alicia Thomas was nervous about this and fearful that her own leadership authority might be compromised, she began to respond to these urges and indeed to nurture them. The result was the emergence of a set of conceptions and commitments – a shared vision, if you will – that laid the platform for what would become the school's mission. (Sergiovanni, 1994: 187–8)

This had been a failing school. It was reopened with a principal who had her own vision. But Sergiovanni still felt there was something missing. It was only when the vision came to be shared that the school really moved forward.

If we contrast the rather sceptical view from Smith about the ethics of a leader getting others to follow her vision with the very positive view we find in Gold and her colleagues or in Sergiovanni, we can see how much will turn on the processes by which vision comes to be shared.

Shared vision and leadership

What does the emphasis on the sharing of vision say about the role of leadership and about the nature of the school in which vision is shared?

First, it certainly says that leadership is not just a matter of the right vision being held by the headteacher, who simply steers everyone else along in the same direction (like the headteacher as taxi driver in the Harber and Davies reading from the previous chapter).

Second, the sharing of vision must be more than just a matter of other people being willing to go along with the fact that the principal is pursuing a certain purpose. In fact we often find, as in the quotation from Gold et al. above, that the sharing of vision is coupled with a sharing of values. The same article mentions 'the spirit of togetherness', a 'shared sense of purpose' and 'we're all pulling in the same direction, sharing the same values' (Gold et al., 2003: 133).

But third, this does not *necessarily* say that the *whole school* is sharing the values and vision. If we read Gold et al. carefully, we see that sometimes what is emphasised (and what is meant, in the context, by the phrase 'we're all pulling in the same direction') is that *the management team* shares the vision and values. Where this happens, it makes leadership a more collective enterprise than leadership by one person, so it is moving in the direction of *distributed leadership*, but not necessarily moving very far in that direction.

Here we are beginning to touch on questions about how the exercise of leadership fits into the *culture* of the school. There are many possibilities, from hierarchical and authoritarian cultures to democratic cultures. In the next two chapters we shall first take a broader look at the idea of school culture, and then look at the ways in which it may be possible for a school to be a *community* in which values and vision are genuinely shared across the whole school.

An alternative vision

To finish this chapter and to give you further ideas to reflect on, I want to refer to some ideas put forward under the title 'An alternative vision' by the American philosopher and educationalist Nel Noddings. Noddings is known for her writing on *caring*. She sees caring as fundamental to the whole of ethics (Noddings, 1984), and because of that, it must, for Noddings, be fundamental to education too. In her book *The Challenge to Care in Schools* (Noddings, 1992) she develops a vision for education that is built on this fundamental ethical commitment of care: a vision that is comprehensive, having something to say about all aspects of education.

Noddings is writing in an American context but there is nothing specifically American about the educational practices to which she wants to offer an alternative. She is particularly concerned about the model of schooling in which the curriculum is dominated by the traditional canon of academic subjects and in which it is assumed that all will follow the same curriculum, so that inevitably, regardless of an individual teacher's intentions, students who do well in the academic subjects are seen to be more successful, better educated, than those who do not. Noddings clearly does not favour this situation, but she also thinks that to find a better alternative we need more than to work differently within the existing system. We need to have a different starting point.

Noddings asks us to engage in a thought experiment. 'Suppose we were raising a very large family of heterogeneous children – children with different biological parents, or mixed races, and widely different talents. How would we want them to turn out? What kind of education would we want for them?' (Noddings, 1992: 45).

Noddings' question is, in effect, a question about the overall aims of education, and as Chapter 2 showed, there are many ways of approaching that question. Later, in Chapter 6, we will see some reason for doubting whether the idea of a family is a helpful metaphor when we are talking about education on a large scale. But certainly the way Noddings poses her questions fits with her fundamental emphasis on caring. Whereas teachers as public servants are not necessarily motivated by care for individual children, Noddings can assume that parents – in an ideal world – are.

She points out that in caring for our children we have to take into account various aspects of their lives: not just their physical health but also their psychological well-being, their opportunities for making their own way in the world in the future, and so on. On this basis she spells out the various elements of her vision for education. First, 'care of the physical self should be a high priority in education' (Nodding, 1992: 48). Then, 'we must be concerned also with the emotional, spiritual and intellectual aspects of self' (p. 49), while 'another basic interest of the self is occupational' (p. 50). But with interpersonal caring as the underlying foundation, we need to give more attention than education usually does to our children's capacities to become involved in intimate caring relationships with others. Then, too, we must take into account their capacity to care for non-human life, to care for objects and instruments (including modern technology), and to care for ideas. It is under this last category that much of the traditional subject matter of education falls.

Even with this brief outline, is already possible to see how the usual priority in education, in which personal and social development come second to intellectual development pursued through the learning of traditional subjects or disciplines, is being reversed here. 'My alternative vision', Noddings writes, 'suggests an entirely different organization of schooling. [This vision] assesses the traditional supremacy of the disciplines as fundamentally wrong. Other matters – centers of care – are more important and more essential to full human life' (Noddings, 1992: 61–2).

It would take a different kind of discussion than is appropriate here to decide whether Noddings' conception of education is really preferable to that which she is criticising. My point in mentioning it is to give an example of a way of thinking about education that seems to merit the term 'vision' as a 'high word'. Noddings is putting forward a conception of education that is to a degree detached from the everyday mundane concerns of schools as they are, because it is asking us to stand back and think of how things could be different. Yet at the same time Noddings' vision is not 'fuzzy'; she devotes her whole book (Noddings, 1992) to discussing in detail what it would involve.

Is this the sort of vision that could possibly be pursued within the existing bureaucratic system? Could even a few aspects of it be pursued? What sort of leadership would be required to pursue elements of this vision?

When governments, or governing bodies of schools, or school boards, use the notion of vision, they will often be taking much of the status quo for granted. Within that constraint, the scope for a working teacher or principal to 'dream dreams and see visions' is necessarily limited. Far from being a 'high word', the idea of vision becomes almost another tool for instrumental purposes.

Perhaps it would be better if we used the word 'vision' rather less in educational discussion and policy-making. Nevertheless, I am not advocating on an individual level that you should refuse to use the word. If you are a principal or aspiring principal, working within a world in which talk of a vision for education has become commonplace, then being willing to go along with that rhetoric, and to make what you can of it, may be just one of the compromises you have to make if you are to work successfully within the system (see the references to Sergiovanni and Bottery above) without being totally constrained by it.

Summary

In this chapter we have examined the notion of vision and its importance in educational leadership. We have looked at three issues in particular: how much scope there is within contemporary educational systems for leaders to pursue an individual vision; whether the notion of vision is too 'fuzzy' to be useful; and whether there is a serious danger of leaders imposing their vision on those they lead.

The upshot of the discussion seems to be, first, that despite the fact that the rhetoric of 'vision' can sound both fuzzy and overblown, we can understand why having a vision, as a conception of a desirable future, is widely seen as a vital aspect of leadership; and, second, that it is important that a vision for an individual school is not imposed but genuinely shared.

The consideration of school culture and community in the next two chapters will help us to see what is involved in the sharing of a vision for a school.

Suggested further reading

Day, C., Harris, A., Hadfield, M., Tolley, H. and Beresford, J. (2000) *Leading Schools in Times of Change*. Buckingham: Open University Press. A report of research on successful school leaders in England, in which one of the research categories is the headteacher's vision and values, as perceived by heads themselves and by teachers, governors, parents and students.

Foreman, K. (1998) 'Vision and mission', in Middlewood, D. and Lumby, J. (eds), *Strategic Management in Schools and Colleges*. London: Paul Chapman. Combines a review of how the idea of vision has become prominent in the discourse of educational leadership, with an assessment of its value.

Sergiovanni, T. (2005) *Strengthening the Heartbeat: Leading and Learning Together in Schools*. San Francisco: Jossey-Bass. See Chapter 3 'Making visions useful'.

Ungoed-Thomas, J. (1996) 'Vision, values and virtues', in Halstead, J. Mark and Taylor, Monica, J. (eds), *Values in Education and Education in Values*. London: Falmer. An English educationalist's view of the relations between vision, values and virtues.

5 | School ethos and culture

In Chapter 3 we looked at the importance in individuals of the kinds of desirable personal qualities that we call *virtues*. At the end of Chapter 1 I had already noted that desirable or undesirable qualities can be attributed to organisations, not just to individuals. We might speak, for instance, of a particular school being a *caring* school (in line with Nel Noddings' vision outlined at the end of Chapter 4). Within a market system, principals may want their schools to be *competitive*. Some principals may want their schools in certain respects to be *democratic*. (I shall say something in the next chapter about how far this is possible.) When we ascribe qualities that we consider desirable or undesirable to a school, not just to the individuals within it, this does not mean the same as saying that all the individuals within the school have that quality. Perhaps a school could be a caring school even if some of the individuals within it – but not too many – lack that quality. When we ascribe desirable or undesirable qualities to an organisation, we are saying something about the *culture* or *ethos* of that organisation.

This chapter will look at the idea of school culture and at the related ideas of climate and ethos. We shall consider how a school leader can influence the culture of his or her school, and we shall also notice the extent to which the culture of a school may reflect the surrounding culture.

This chapter will help you to:

- be aware of how the terms 'ethos' and 'culture' are used in educational research;
- be able to reflect on the relationship between school culture and values;
- understand some of the factors that influence the culture of a school, and consider how far leaders can change these factors.

There are four main sections in this chapter: ethos, climate and culture; ethos and culture in the context of values; school culture and leadership; and school culture and the surrounding culture. The second section includes three case studies.

Ethos, climate and culture

Write down some sentences, referring to your school or another school you know, in which it seems natural to you to use one of the words 'culture', 'climate', or 'ethos'.

Which of these terms would you use in talking about the values that characterise – or that you would wish to characterise – the institution in which you work? Do you see any difference between these three terms?

In the everyday discourse of teachers and school leaders it is unlikely that there is any very systematic distinction to be made between the three terms 'culture', 'climate' and 'ethos'. This may also be true of the discourse of educational research, but a study of the literature by Glover and Coleman (2005) suggests that there are some differences and that it might be helpful to build on these differences. (There is a general point here about trying to use language in a way that will be an aid to clear thinking. If there is no distinction worth making between the ideas that are marked by different words, then using more than one word risks confusion. If there are important distinctions to be made, then it is worth trying to use different terms consistently to mark the difference.)

Of these three terms, the notion of ethos seems to be the one most directly associated with values. This is partly because ethos emerges as being the most concerned with subjective factors that seem to be important to the life of a school but are hard to characterise objectively or to measure. But the apparent direct association with values may also arise because ethos is the term that schools often use explicitly when they want to talk about their values. Two examples, referred to by Glover and Coleman, are given below.

Educational researchers need to be able to look at features that they can measure. They will sometimes try to measure aspects of a school's culture, using that term, but Glover and Coleman suggest that in the research literature 'climate' tends to be used of features of a school that are measurable (the nature of a school's intake, truancy rates, number of exclusions and so on) rather than features that can only be grasped in a qualitative, perhaps impressionistic, way.

Ethos: two examples

Here are two examples of the way that particular schools explicitly see their ethos.

Kgaswe Primary School (Botswana)

SCHOOL ETHOS

The Kgaswe Primary School motto 'Know Thyself' forms the basis of our School Ethos.

We at Kgaswe Primary School believe in:

- a commitment to the school's ethos of excellence and quality
- honesty, integrity and polite conduct
- tolerance and empathy
- trust and respect
- encouraging leadership and team spirit
- providing pupils with the skills to be international citizens.

These collective principles guide the thoughts and actions of the staff and pupils at Kgaswe Primary School.

(From http://www.geocities.com/kgaswe/ethos.htm)

The Dales School (England)

At the Dales School we aim to establish an ethos characterised by a spirit of consensus built on clear and effective management. Each member of the school community, including pupils, should feel valued and able to share ideas and feelings through open communication and mutual support.

In more detail, the characteristics of the school ethos will include the following qualities:

- the right of the individual to equal regard and opportunities;
- the ability to meet the needs of pupils in an analytical and sensitive manner and to seek to improve skills and resources to make the school community more effective;
- a willingness to discuss issues and concerns in a spirit of security, honesty and openness;
- the transferring of information and the sharing of ideas with an awareness of preconceptions and prejudices;
- the fostering of attitudes and values which work for the good of the community while recognising the needs of the individual;
- an awareness of how others feel and a willingness to offer or seek help in a confidential manner, as appropriate;
- a recognition of the value of working within a team and the ability to resolve conflicts of ideas and values;
- a willingness to take responsibility for our own actions;
- being prepared to keep things in perspective often through a sense of humour.

The ethos of a school will have a direct effect on pupils' spiritual, moral and emotional development. Many of the rules which might be associated with the characteristics outlined above, such as 'tell the truth', are, as far as they relate to pupils, covered in the Personal and Social Education Curriculum.

Non-verbal communication, including body language, is very important and one of the main skills involved in effective listening.

(From http://www.thedalesschool.org/?Vok=8)

These are two explicit statements of *ethos*. The schools would have been less likely to use the terms 'climate' or 'culture' for these statements. 'Ethos' is a term that organisations often use about themselves when referring to their own perception of their values. 'Climate' and 'culture' perhaps are researchers' terminology, more likely to be used by observers looking at a school from the outside. This would fit with the fact that 'climate' and 'culture' are used in association with more objective and measurable factors, since researchers need to have such factors to work with.

However, while a particular ethos may be what schools explicitly attribute to themselves, it is arguable that the actual culture of a school may be more important when we are looking at the values of a school. We shall look at culture in more detail in this chapter.

Ethos and culture in the context of values

When schools explicitly state their values, and when researchers study the values of schools, it will often in effect be *principles* that are the focus of attention, even if that word is not used. Principles can be stated explicitly, and at least to some extent one can observe whether a school is following its own stated principles or not; indeed a school can observe this for itself. Glover and Coleman refer to a study by Glover and Law (2004) which showed that 'the most successful schools, as judged by pupil outcomes and stakeholder support, are those that have a clearly stated set of values that are monitored to ensure that they are fundamental to policy and practice' (Glover and Coleman, 2005: 259).

When considering the qualities of individuals in Chapter 3, we saw the importance of thinking not only about the principles that individuals subscribe to, but also about the more complex qualities of persons that philosophers increasingly refer to as *virtues*. We can say that institutions too can have *virtues*. A school can be just or unjust, tolerant or intolerant, compassionate or lacking in compassion. To ascribe such qualities to a school is not necessarily to say that any particular individuals in a school have these qualities; it is to make an evaluation of the practices and procedures of the school. As in the case of individuals, where it is easy to know what principles they say they subscribe to but quite difficult to be sure of any judgement about their virtues, so in the case of institutions it is easy to see what principles they claim to follow but more difficult to be sure about their virtues. We sometimes think we recognise in an 'intuitive' way the differences in character between one individual and another – though our judgement may not be very reliable – and in a similar 'intuitive' way we may think we recognise a difference in the qualities of one school compared with another. People speak of being aware of the atmosphere of a particular school after a very brief experience of it. Researchers are often trying to find some way of making such subjective judgements measurable.

In the case of individuals we sometimes recognise a discrepancy between the principles they subscribe to and their practice. Someone may talk a lot about tolerance but not actually appear to be a tolerant person in practice; we could say he subscribes to a *principle* of tolerance but lacks the *virtue* of tolerance. In the case of institutions as well, it is sometimes possible to see a mismatch between principle and practice. Thus Glover and Coleman cite Carter (2002) who 'shows how a school that is attempting to ensure the twin aims of inclusivity and equality as fundamental features of its ethos is also still prompting and permitting behaviours that run counter to this, by maintaining cultural practices that are not embedded in the value system of the school' (Glover and Coleman, 2005: 258–9).

This illustrates well one of the differences in the way the terms 'ethos' and 'culture' are used. There is an explicitly intended ethos that is undermined by the actual culture of the school. Culture still has to do with values; indeed many discussions of school culture refer to attitudes, values and practices. But people are not always so consciously aware of the culture within which they live and work as they are of the professed ethos of their school. This less conscious and deliberate aspect of culture is well captured in this summary from Peterson and Deal:

> ... the underground stream of norms, values, beliefs, traditions, and rituals that has built up over time as people work together, solve problems, and confront challenges. This set of informal expectations and values shapes how people think, feel and act in schools. This highly enduring web of influence binds the school together and makes it special. (Peterson and Deal, 1998, cited in Glover and Coleman, 2005).

Read the following case (a fictionalised one supplied by Derek Glover). Consider whether the culture described fits the general conception of a school culture just quoted from Glover and Coleman. What do you think would be an appropriate course of action for the new headteacher?

Case study: Sweetbriar School

Sweetbriar School is a boys' denominational school set up by a missionary group in East Africa. The local inspectors have recently visited the school and feel that it is not serving the area as well as it could. There are several indicators that things are not right – public examination results have fallen recently, attendance has also dropped and there have been significant discipline problems. The local community are aware of the problems but the staff feel that they are being misjudged and that there has been a fall in the calibre of students.

The view of local community representatives, advisory group and staff was that the school was being judged unfairly. 'It is no good them coming in from outside when they don't know our problems,' said Father Moses, the chairman of the advisory group and senior member of the associated mission. Teachers have been interviewed on local radio and argue that 'our staff face an impossible task, traditional values such as respect have been undermined and we can no longer run things in a way that was previously successful.' They were particularly resentful of criticism of the continuation of a 'hard' regime and argued that a measure of corporal punishment was in the interests of the boys because they 'know where they are'.

The inspectors had referred to the 'prevailing macho culture' of the school. This had been shown in the relationship between staff and boys with 'continuing use of surnames, a lack of courtesies such as please and thank you, and in the prevailing untidiness of the buildings.' The headteacher was aware of these comments but felt that those who were looking at the school had failed to understand that boys were 'used to the rough and tumble of the male-dominated society which is all around them'. The headteacher, in an attempt to disprove much of the criticism, then invited a researcher from a college of higher education to interview students throughout the school. The interviewer worked with a group of boys from each of the years and reported as follows:

> The boys say that you have to be tough to survive in this school. They mention the intimidation that often occurs when older boys want younger boys to be part of their gang outside school, and to ensure that they will conform to prevailing attitudes to staff, work and social activities. They speak of the need to be hard, especially if you are to survive, e.g. in physical education lessons, and in those lessons where personal opinion has to conform to the norm for the local area. Staff may be told of problems, and there is evidence of the existence of policies, but the boys say that little action is taken and that they suffer in the long term if they make a fuss.

It was, said the report, regrettable that 78 per cent of those interviewed stated that school life was unhappy, and only 30 per cent felt that they stood any chance of completing their course because parents felt that scarce money was being wasted. The conclusion to the report included references to 'softening the culture, enhancing the relationship between staff and boys, developing an encouraging rather than an intimidating atmosphere, and insisting on basic courtesies in relationships, language and behaviour'.

This was a severe shock to both the chairman of the advisory group and the head, who recalled that the school had turned out many people who as pillars of the local community had done much to show that the values and training provided by the school in the past had been to their advantage in a developing community. The comment of Father Moses was that 'the school will have to change to meet new expectations, but we are being asked to do the impossible – once we drop our defences the boys will have the upper hand.'

Part of the problem represented in this case study is that different parties have rather different perceptions of the culture of the school. We could also speak here of the ethos of the school, but it seems likely that the ethos intended by the head, advisory group and staff, with their reference to traditional values, is rather different from the actual culture as described by the researcher.

Part of the task of a new head might be to try to improve the culture of the school. There are difficulties about that idea, for two reasons. First, the culture of an organisation necessarily involves many people, so that one person alone cannot change the culture independently of the others. We shall look later at how far a head can deliberately change the culture of a school.

Second, no school is isolated from the culture of the surrounding society. The surrounding culture will influence the culture within the school in more or less obvious ways. This influence may be welcome, if it supports what the school wants to do, and far less welcome if it works in the opposite direction. The influence of the surrounding culture on the internal culture of a school is illustrated in the next case study.

Case study: St Martins, Uganda

This is a case of an actual school in Uganda, reported by Robina Mirembe and Lynn Davies (2001). They describe the surrounding culture in Uganda as being heavily paternalistic, and see this culture as reflected – and indeed reproduced – within the school. The general topic of relations between school culture and its surrounding culture is one we shall come back to at the end of this chapter. For the moment, we can draw out just a few of the aspects of the school culture on which Mirembe and Davies focus. St Martins largely serves a professional elite, and while it is a government school it is also a boarding school and seems to aspire to something of the ethos of the traditional English 'public school'. It was a boys' school until the 1930s, when it became coeducational, though the ratio of boys to girls is still 3:1. 'However, in its culture St Martins can still be seen as a boys' school to which girls have been admitted, rather than a fully mixed school' (Mirembe and Davies, 2001: 403). The male-dominated ethos is reflected in the leadership of the school, not just in the actual composition of the senior management, but also in the qualities expected of leaders. 'Qualities such as toughness and firmness, according to a senior male teacher, were found among male teachers only' (Mirembe and Davies, 2001: 405–6).

Within the traditional boarding school pattern, there was a leadership structure among students also, namely a prefect system. While prefect positions were open to boys and girls, the system and the general expectations were biased against girls attaining or even aspiring to these positions. 'One classic illustration at St Martins was the student "interviews" for aspiring prefects, where of the interviewing panel of 40 pupils, 38 were boys' (Mirembe and Davies, 2001: 404).

Mirembe and Davies go on to point out some further dire consequences of the gender imbalance in power. Their article is part of a larger study of AIDS education in Uganda. They find that although there is a curriculum that teaches messages about sexual behaviour aimed at preventing HIV/AIDS, the actual culture of the school tends to undermine these messages. In short, girls are subject to serious sexual harassment within a power culture that can make it difficult to say no. What actually happens in the school tends, contrary to the official position, to perpetuate the sexual culture outside the school.

Throughout their paper Mirembe and Davies are using the term 'culture' in a way compatible with the account quoted above from Peterson and Deal. A stream of norms, values, beliefs, traditions and rituals, shaping how people think, feel and act, is the sort of thing that Mirembe and Davies are talking about.

But what is very striking about this example is that this school culture seems in all sorts of ways an undesirable one. We need to remember that beliefs can be false or ill-founded, and norms and values, traditions and rituals, can themselves be evaluated; if we uphold values of fairness, equity and the importance of self-esteem, we can criticise many of the values and traditions that are evident in this school.

The only part of Peterson and Deal's account that does not seem to fit the present case is the final sentence quoted: 'This highly enduring web of influence binds the school together and makes it special.' The web of influence investigated by Mirembe and Davies may in one way bind the school together in that it discourages female students and staff from being too openly critical, but in another way, far from binding everyone into a set of shared values, it splits the school population into opposing groups. If this culture 'makes the school special' it is in a way that the leadership would not want openly to endorse, though even they tend to go along with it. On a wider view, the internal school culture does not make the school special at all, since it only reflects wider cultural norms.

These two examples, fictional and real, make it clear that school leaders cannot afford to neglect the culture of their school. It is also true that the role of headteacher or school principal is potentially such a pivotal one that the way that role is filled – the characteristics of the person filling it and the way they go about their job – is always liable to make some difference to the culture of a school. This difference may or may not be intentional. The next case shows some of the ways in which the difference made to a school by the head may not be deliberately planned by that person.

Case study: Cerberus School

Cerberus School (not its real name), in the Midlands of England, went through a difficult period in which three people held the role of headteacher within three years. Busher and Barker (2003b) report that:

> The personalities of and interpersonal relationships generated by senior staff in the school, especially the headteachers, were important mediating factors in how people in the school responded to the external pressures on them, and helped to create particular cultures in the school. The three headteachers who led Cerberus through the period of this study adopted contrasting styles and were perceived by colleagues and students as professional leaders of quite different stamps.

The following is an edited version of the comparison:

The Old Head was seen to have a negative attitude, developed during a long period in post. He was head at Cerberus for 22 years. A teacher governor said that colleagues were humiliated at meetings if they questioned any aspect of current policy. A head of year remembered that parents found him rude, while children disliked his gloomy presence in assemblies and about the school. He discouraged clubs and educational visits that might have disrupted the routine operations of the school and delegated work and responsibility to a hard-pressed deputy and the heads of department. The Old Head's approach was visible in coercive actions that discouraged initiative and participation. Children were locked out of the school at lunchtime; staff were not allowed to participate in local education networks; parents with complaints were referred to the deputy head; the governors met on an ad hoc basis with no established committees or procedures.

The Acting Head was 15 years younger than his predecessor and presented as self-confident, positive and above all successful. Parents later remembered that he was 'a very loveable man ... incredibly open, excitable, boyish, lots of humour, loads of energy and *joie de vivre*'. Pupils were swept along by his enthusiasm, while staff morale was said to have risen because 'he made people feel valued'. The Acting Head was described as a coach or trainer who specialised in building teams and boosting morale. He set out to arouse a positive response. Passion and praise were prominent at the informal morning staff briefings and in assemblies. Colleagues remembered that he used the term 'brilliant' to describe almost any constructive effort. Although he encouraged many staff, however, he also upset others by dealing ruthlessly with people he considered to be less effective.

The career path of the New Head combined elements from each of the others. Although he had retired early after twenty years as headteacher at a school in another authority, his length of service was seen positively. He was seen as knowing how to carry things through, honest but a political operator – a strategist, clear about where he could put his energies. He knew how to recognise influential people and how to get them on board. The staff were encouraged by his enthusiasm and work rate, though some were anxious about the demands he made on staff. Students warmed to his consistency and fairness, and staff recognised his desire to increase responsibility through having decisions made jointly. People recognised that he wanted to 'shift the culture from blaming staff to a supportive, collaborative one'.

This study shows three different individuals who clearly make a difference to the culture of the school. But only the new head is explicitly said to be trying to 'shift the culture'. We need to look further at how far the changing of a school culture is something that can be quite deliberately undertaken. It is clear enough that it cannot be done overnight and that in some sense the changes that a head tries to bring about have to carry the staff, or at least most of the staff, with them or the culture change will not come about at all – not, at any rate, the kind of change intended. But what in practice is the head to do?

Do you consider that, in a leadership role, you might be able to take steps deliberately to change the culture of a school? What might such steps be?

School culture and leadership

David Hargreaves (1999) has suggested a systematic approach to changing a school's culture. As he points out, trying to bring the change about is just one task among three that have to be undertaken. First is to diagnose the present culture of the school. For this it is useful to have some classificatory scheme; several such schemes are mentioned in Hargreaves' chapter, and there are more in the wider literature on school leadership. Second is to decide in what ways one wants the culture to change. Only when these two tasks have been completed is it time for the task that Hargreaves calls *managerial*, of devising and implementing a strategy for moving the school's culture in the desired direction.

Of these three tasks it is the second – which Hargreaves calls *directional* – that most obviously calls on a sense of values. A particular sense of the desirable culture for a school could be part of a wider vision for the future of the school. Interestingly, it is the task that Hargreaves says least about. But he does point out that it is not necessarily best for a school's culture to be 'clear, consistent and consensual'. A certain amount of dissent and ambiguity can, he suggests, be healthy. This is something to keep in mind when we look in the next chapter at the idea of the school as a community.

Much of Hargreaves' discussion is devoted to practical moves by which a school leader might try to move a school in the desired direction. The leader, for instance, will select the most appropriate leadership style. The idea of leadership styles has been much discussed in the literature on school leadership (so that there is no need to go into the characteristics of different styles in detail here), and a variety of styles have been distinguished by different writers. The following list is derived from Leithwood and colleagues (1999):

Instructional
Transformational
Moral
Participative
Managerial
Contingent

You have seen something of different leadership styles in the case study of Ceberus School above. In that example, the leadership style of a particular individual seems largely to be a function of the individual's personality. But what is found in some of the management literature, including Hargreaves' discussion of culture change, is the idea that a style can be quite deliberately chosen. And it can be chosen in order to promote a culture change that again is deliberately aimed at.

It is worth reflecting on the way that culture is being used here – I mean both the way the *word* 'culture' is being used and also, more importantly, the way that the phenomenon itself is being used. For Hargreaves is not using the word to denote something rather indefinable that exists in the background of people's activities and that may take many years to develop: the *stream of norms, values, beliefs, traditions and rituals, shaping how people think, feel and act* that I quoted above. For Hargreaves the culture of a school appears to be something that is much more deliberately malleable and so in a sense closer to the surface. It is actually something that can itself be *used* as a management tool. Might there be a danger here of the same sort of manipulation that Michael Smith feared, as we saw in the previous chapter? I do not think Hargreaves intends it this way but, if there is not complete transparency among the staff about what is being done, deliberately changing a culture *could* involve using people as a means towards an end, where the end in mind is to produce a certain sort of culture and the kind of culture is itself a means towards a further end – the successful school.

It is interesting to compare Hargreaves' chapter with the following chapter in the same book (Prosser, 1999). This is 'Primary teaching as a culture of care' by Jennifer Nias. Nias cites Noddings, and her view of primary school culture does have affinities with that of Noddings. She certainly does not think that teachers should see themselves as part of a culture of care in an unreflective or uncritical way. But there is a sense in Nias of the way a certain school culture can stem from a deep ethical commitment rather than being a tool to be used instrumentally.

In Chapter 3 we looked at the qualities that individual leaders may have: they may for instance subscribe to certain principles or show certain virtues. In this chapter we have been paying attention to similar points about schools. The comparison between the perspectives on the individual and on the school may raise a question of priorities: which is more important, the values of the head of a school, or the values of the school itself as shown in its ethos and culture? This question sets up an exaggerated contrast. Certainly it is not a straight either/or situation, where what is important is *either* the qualities of the leader *or* the qualities of the school as an institution. The position is rather that, once the importance of the values operating within a school as an institution is recognised, a different set of questions has to be asked about individual leadership: not what are the desirable qualities of the educational leader, but how does the role of leadership have to be conceived if desirable values are to be fostered as part of the shared ethos and culture of a school?

If there are to be values widely shared throughout the school, and if people in the school are to be working together towards a common goal, then any authoritarian notion of a single leader in charge of everything that goes on cannot be adequate. In some way leadership has to get away from the feeling of 'them and us' and work towards a 'spirit of togetherness' (Gold et al., 2003: 133). This may still be compatible with a variety of learning styles, but not with the most purely 'managerial' of styles.

It is worth reflecting further on why this is so. What is it about managerial leadership that makes it less appropriate for an educational community in which values are shared and common goals pursued? In thinking about this you will find some of the ideas in Chapter 4 relevant: look back particularly at the discussion of Michael Smith's article. In effect he was arguing that the managerial style inevitably treats people as means to the manager's own ends, making other people subordinate to the values that the manager is pursuing (even if these values seem to be good ones). Any school that is to function as a community of shared educational values – a notion we shall look at further in the next chapter – has to get away from a purely managerial style.

School culture and the surrounding culture

The present chapter has been mostly about culture in the sense of the internal culture of a school rather than the wider culture of the surrounding society. But we saw in the case study from Mirembe and Davies that the internal culture of the school may closely reflect the wider culture. Busher and Barker, too, in their discussion of Cerberus School, have a lot to say about the effects of the wider culture. The nature of the wider culture is always *likely* to be reflected in the internal culture of the school. People's experiences in one area of their lives often influence their expectations about other areas. For example, if people have experienced authoritarian modes of decision-making within the family and in the workplace they may expect similar patterns to prevail within schools. Another widespread case is that gender assumptions in the wider society are reflected in assumptions about leadership within a school. The study by Mirembe and Davies gives evidence of this, as does a study in China that asked senior teachers about gender and leadership, leading to responses such as: 'Sometimes male leaders have strong abilities and are brave and act quickly and are wise. Female leaders are reluctant and hesitant' and 'Women are careful and cautious and too kind which is not appropriate' (Coleman et al., 1998: 151).

Though a school culture will tend to correspond in several respects to the surrounding culture, a school that takes its responsibilities, its moral purpose, seriously, will often need to a degree to distance itself from that wider culture. Sexism is just one case of an aspect of the wider culture that would be better not reproduced. Another is violence. In 2005 the first holder of the post of Children's Commissioner in England said that he found violence to be pervasive in English culture. 'I have no doubt that children are being brought up in a society where violence is the norm. I include in this the violence on television, in the workplace and in the home' (Hill, 2005: 10). It could be debated whether violence is quite as prevalent as the commissioner finds, but it is surely clear that in so far as the wider culture is violent, this is something that schools can and should try to counteract – as many do, for instance through anti-bullying policies.

More difficult to counteract is the commercialism of the wider society: the fact that firms driven by the bottom line of the profit motive are constantly pushing conceptions of a desirable lifestyle that may not be good either for individuals in the short term or for the planet in the slightly longer term, conceptions that in any case are liable to distract young people from some of the values and aims of their schools. No doubt some restraint is put on commercial activities either through the law or through a sense of social responsibility on the part of some business people; how far this is so will vary from one country to another. (See Brighouse (2006: 49–50) for a comment on the commercialism of the United States, and Bottery (2004) for a view of the global picture.) The question here is how far schools should seek to work directly counter to the commercial culture. If they do decide to do that, there is little doubt that their room for manoeuvre is limited, given the extent to which aspects of the market culture – competition between schools, the need to attract students – have pervaded the world of education. As Bottery's book makes clear, this is one of the major challenges facing educational leaders today.

Summary

In this chapter we considered the relationship between school ethos and school culture (with lesser attention also to school climate). We went on to look at the importance of school culture in particular, and looked at a detailed example from Uganda in which the internal culture of a school was clearly influenced by the wider culture of the society. We also recognised that the style and personality of individual leaders can have a strong influence on the culture of a school. We asked how far a school's culture can be directly under the control of a leader.

Suggested further reading

Busher, H. and Barker, B. (2003a) 'The crux of leadership: shaping school culture by contesting the policy contexts and practices of teaching and learning', *Educational Management and Administration*, 31 (1): 51–65. A report of research on how the surrounding culture of educational policy affects the internal culture of three English urban schools.

Hargreaves, A. (1994) *Changing Teachers, Changing Times: Teachers' Work and Culture in the Postmodern Age*. London: Cassell. An influential book and source of a typology of four teaching cultures: individualism; collaboration; contrived collegiality; and Balkanisation.

Prosser, J. (ed.) (1999) *School Culture*. London: Paul Chapman. A useful collection of papers, including the chapter by David Hargreaves referred to in this chapter. Also good in understanding the nature of school culture are the chapters by Jon Prosser, 'The evolution of school culture research', and Louise Stoll, 'School culture: black hole or fertile ground for school improvement?' The chapter by Jennifer Nias, 'Primary teaching as a culture of care', is of particular interest in relation to values.

6 | Community and democracy

In the previous chapter we looked at the notion of culture. In everyday discourse the notions of culture and community are often linked. We often identify a group of people as being a community because they are conceived to share a culture. Here the term 'community' is functioning in a value-neutral way. (For example, we could speak of a community of people united by their hostile attitude towards outsiders; we do not have to approve of the way people live just because they are a community.) We may also use the term 'community' in a neutral way when we talk about the relations between a school and its surrounding community.

On the other hand, if a principal says that her school is a community (perhaps 'a real community') she is probably not making a neutral sociological observation (which would be true of any school), but means to convey a positive evaluation: saying that the school has some desirable features that would not be shared by just any school. Many schools like to think of themselves as communities. And they like too to have close links with their surrounding communities. What are the values of community that schools hope to realise in these ways? Are there any risks in emphasising the importance of community? And is a particular form of leadership – a democratic form – most suitable for schools that aspire to be communities?

This chapter will help you to:

- appreciate the values that may be inherent in community, but also possible drawbacks;
- understand what may be involved in a school being a community;
- appreciate connections between community and democracy;
- reflect on the extent to which democratic forms of leadership are possible and desirable within schools.

This chapter has three main sections: community and shared values; community and democracy; and democratic leadership.

Consider first what the notion of 'a community' means to you. Try to write a definition. Do you find that you need different definitions for different kinds of community?

Community and shared values

'Community' may be a partly geographical term, referring to the people living close to each other and interacting with each other within a particular area, such as a village or a neighbourhood within a town.

But it may also suggest a set of people – who don't necessarily know each other or live in the same area – who are picked out as having something in common that differentiates them from other groups in the society. The something in common may be a religious belief (Muslim community, Catholic community), origin or ethnicity (European community, Asian community), a way of life dependent on the surroundings (rural community, inner-city community), sexual orientation (the gay community), an interest and occupation (the scientific community, the artistic community), and so on through other examples.

All of these are ways in which the term 'community' is often used, but none of these so far does much to pick out the way in which a school might be a community. If members of a community have to be living together, this would not apply to schools apart from residential (boarding) schools. If members of a community have to share certain beliefs, or a certain way of life, or certain personal characteristics or interests, then on such a basis many schools will not be communities though some may be (for instance, a faith-based school might be a community because of a shared commitment to certain beliefs, but the members of a secular school might not have anything equivalent to such beliefs that they all share).

Nevertheless, looking for what is shared across a school may be a fruitful way of thinking about how a school can be a community.

What kinds of shared values, beliefs or commitments, apart from religious ones, might be sufficient to make us think of a school as a community?

It may be tempting to say – as people often do – that shared values make a community. But not just any values will do. If our values are what matter to us, then there will be many things that matter to us that have only a tenuous connection with community.

You may remember from Chapter 1 that Kenneth Strike and his co-authors used 'pickles are better than olives' as an example of a value judgement. That may have been too trivial, or too much a pure matter of taste, to be a good example of a value judgement. But we should not go to the opposite extreme of thinking that values cannot be about things that are material and mundane.

In another place – in one of two very useful articles that he has written on schools as communities – Strike says: 'Most people in schools value good plumbing, but few robust school communities are likely to be formed on this basis' (Strike, 2000: 618). This is not a trivial example, because there is a deeper value – physical health – that is supported by good plumbing. Good plumbing arrangements are important for any group of people who will be living or working together in close proximity. But there is nothing about plumbing that makes it any more valuable to people engaged in education than to people engaged in any other activity.

So if we are to say that shared values are important in making a school into a community, we can look to values that have some distinctive connection with education. Strike's own view, put in the language we explored above in Chapter 4, is that what makes a school a community is a shared educational vision. He says, for example, 'School communities ... will have substantive commitments about the nature of a good education, rooted in at least a partial conception of what constitutes human flourishing' (Strike, 2000: 624).

In Chapter 4 we considered the possible disadvantages of one individual trying to push through his or her personal vision. Now we can revisit the idea of vision again by asking what is involved in a school having a shared educational vision.

In a particular school it might be that everyone agrees on certain values that do have something specifically to do with teaching and learning: perhaps everyone thinks it is important that the students in the school get good exam results. This would give the members of the school a shared aim, but (I argued at the beginning of Chapter 4) to have an aim or purpose is still not necessarily to have a vision. 'Vision' implies a fuller, richer picture of how a school should be. This is bringing us closer to what Strike has in mind. In a different place he puts it this way:

> When a school has a shared educational project, it has a vision of the education it wishes to provide which is known to and agreed upon by the members of the community. This vision is rooted in a common vision of human flourishing, and it involves aims that cannot be achieved without cooperation. This shared educational project is the basis of the community's self-understanding, and is the basis for articulating roles within the community. It grounds the community's educational practices, rituals and traditions, grounds the community's governance practices, and is the basis of the community's ability to achieve the goods of community such as belonging, loyalty, mutual identification, and trust. (Strike, 2003: 74).

Central to this understanding of a shared educational project is the idea of a 'common vision of human flourishing'. To understand what this means you may find it helpful to know a little of the context of recent philosophy of education in which Strike's work is set. In Chapter 2, when I tried to pull together a variety of ideas about the aims of education, I took it as basic that education is meant in one way or another to make people's lives better. Philosophers often express this by saying that the ultimate aim of education is 'the good life' or 'human flourishing'. But what kind of life is a good life? Is it a life of as much material comfort as possible? A life of service to others? A life of devotion to God? A fulfilling personal and family life? Clearly there are many different ideas of a good life that different people are attached to.

In modern societies we often take this variety of conceptions of a good life for granted. It is part of the pluralism of modern societies. To some extent at least it seems that people can live together in the same society even though they have very different ideas of what kind of life is most worth living (we have to say 'to some extent', because there are also many examples where this kind of peaceful coexistence doesn't happen or is not stable).

If a school within a large plural society is a microcosm of that society – if it contains within it people who more or less randomly represent a whole range of the ideas of human flourishing that are present across the whole society – then such a school will not have a shared conception of human flourishing any more than the whole society does. So when Strike speaks of a shared idea of human flourishing it appears he cannot be speaking of that kind of school.

Contrast the 'social microcosm' kind of school with a school that is set up by a religious community in order to promote the beliefs and ideals of that community. Then that school will have a shared conception of human flourishing, reflecting the shared conception in the wider religious community. Such a school, it seems, will itself be a community whereas the microcosm school will not be.

Why is it good for a school to be a community?

Strike (2003: 72–3) lists – and expands on – seven reasons why it may be good for a school to be a community:

1. It is important in providing an emotionally secure learning environment.
2. It supports the internalization of the norms involved in learning.
3. It supports a sense of equality between students.
4. It may prevent the school becoming fragmented into subcultures.
5. It helps to develop trust and cooperation.
6. As a result of trust and cooperation, it helps reduce bureaucracy.
7. It fosters non-alienated learning.

But the case for schools as communities of shared values is not one-sided. There is room for different views about how desirable it is that a school should have a shared conception of human flourishing in the way a religious community does.

Your own view may be influenced by your own experience and by the kinds of school you have worked in. You may think that it is a good thing for people in a school to be working and sharing their experiences with others who take similar views, so that they will all be supporting each other in pursuing the same idea of a good life. On the other hand you may think that it is better if people in a school are mixing with others who have quite different ideas about human flourishing – after all, that is what the wider society is like, and schools should surely be preparing people for life in that wider plural society.

In what follows keep in mind that there are issues in question here that are far from just academic. There are real political issues in many parts of the world about how far it is good for schools to be made up of people who in some way are all of a kind, or whether it is better that each school contains a mix of all kinds of people. In Britain, as I write, there is very lively debate over the merits of faith schools. In terms both of academic results and internal ethos they often seem to be attractive to parents, but other people are worried that the existence of faith schools will militate against cohesion across different groups in society. As with any complex issue, setting up oversimple contrasts is unlikely to be helpful. But we should certainly recognise, as Strike does, that community can bring with it 'bads' as well as 'goods'. Strike emphasises the dilemma about *inclusiveness*: if a school is to consist only of people who share a common conception of what is good for human beings, then it cannot contain a cross-section of the whole of society, because society as a whole does not share a common conception of what is good for human beings. So such a school has to be selective in some way. By the very fact that it seeks to build and maintain a community of shared values and beliefs, it has to exclude some people.

Let's ask, then, just how much *has* to be shared if a school is to have a shared vision? Does such a vision have to rest in an overall vision of a good life, such as may be found in (some) religious communities? Or can it be something less far-reaching than this, which can still give a vision of life *in the school*? And can it be something that unites people in their vision *of education*, even if they do not share the same vision for the whole of life?

There are various possibilities between saying, at one extreme, that all that is needed for a community to exist is some sort of shared values (which, as the plumbing example shows, is not true), and saying, at the other extreme, that a school is not a community at all unless the people in it share a whole worldview, an overall vision of a good life. We can see more of these intermediate possibilities by looking at four metaphors of community that Strike picks out (Strike, 2003: 74–6).

As you read about these metaphors, consider which ones are viable metaphors for schools as communities.

Metaphors of community

The first metaphor is the school as a *tribe*. In a tribe, as Strike is perhaps imagining it, people share a whole way of life; they perhaps have little individuality and little privacy (or desire for it).

The second metaphor is the school as *congregation*. The name reflects the religious context in which this model is most at home, where members constitute a community because they share certain beliefs or worldview. The beliefs or worldviews in question are ones that are important across many areas of life, but at the same time they do not determine everything about how the members of a community live. Muslims do not all live the same kind of life, in all respects, just because they are Muslims, or Christians just because they are Christians. (Among people sharing a religion, some live urban lives, some rural; some live technologically sophisticated lives, and others simpler lives; some are entrepreneurs while others devote their lives to public service; and so on.) So a community that is constituted by the sharing of beliefs may be inclusive of quite a wide range of people and lifestyles, but at the same time it can't fully include people who do not share the beliefs.

Next is the metaphor of the school as a *family*. It is worth giving some attention to this metaphor because many people (perhaps especially in primary education) are attracted by the idea of a school as a large family. Think back to the account of Nel Noddings' vision for education at the end of Chapter 4. Was her ideal that of the school as being as much like a family as possible? Possibly there is something of the same metaphor operating when Nias (1999) describes how a primary-school culture could revolve around caring. Even someone like Hodgkinson, who is thoroughly realistic in recognising the bureaucratic nature of any actual school system, once recommended the idea of a school as a family (Hodgkinson, 1991: 61).

Last in Strike's scheme is the school as an *orchestra* or *guild*. Members of an orchestra share in the practice of making music; this gives them a reason for cooperating *while they are functioning as an orchestra*. But outside of that context they may be quite different people with different beliefs and lifestyles. They have private lives that have nothing to do with their work as orchestral players.

Which of these are viable metaphors for schools as communities? The metaphor of a tribe, where almost everything is shared, can hardly be a viable metaphor for a school unless, perhaps, it is a small residential school.

Another metaphor that is questionable in a school context is that of the family. Though many people find the idea attractive, we should think about how far the comparison can really be taken. What is distinctive of a family as a kind of community?

First, it *can* be that a family is held together by particularly close emotional bonds. But we should consider whether these are really the sorts of emotional bonds that are appropriate among teachers, or among students, or between teachers and students, in a school. For one thing, family bonds are not always equally strong among all members of a family. There can be all sorts of personal difficulties and tensions within a family, and parents may favour one child over another. In these respects, at least, actual families are not a good model for schools.

Second, although there *may* be strong emotional bonds, a family as such does not necessarily share values or share a common goal. For these reasons Strike does not think the family is the most appropriate metaphor for a school as a community, and he is not alone in this. David Hargreaves makes the same point (1999: 58). Bottery (2004: ch. 9) agrees, in a discussion of educational community in which he refers to Strike (2003).

Strike thinks that the metaphor of the school as an orchestra or guild is a viable one, as is the metaphor of the school as a congregation. These two metaphors have in common that the school has a shared educational vision that can act as the 'social glue' holding the community together. This vision may be deeply connected with beliefs and worldviews, as can happen in a faith school, or it may go less deep but still be a coherent goal that is important to all the members of the group – like the goal of music-making for an orchestra. This last example suggests that there might in a school be a shared conception of what a good education is, without necessarily a deep shared understanding about everything that makes for a flourishing human life.

Some real-world questions

While metaphors can be very helpful to our thinking, it is time to ask some questions about the real world of education. First, how far and in what ways is it actually desirable that schools should function as communities? At bottom this is, of course, a question about values. If we want schools to be communities, that is presumably because we think there are certain desirable features of communities that we also think are desirable in schools. But not everything about communities is necessarily positive; as we have seen, Strike emphasises that a school that is a community may exclude those who do not fit in. We have to weigh up whether the benefits of community outweigh the disadvantages.

Despite some differences on the notion of the school as a community, the idea that there should in a school be a shared educational purpose – which is arguably the central point of Strike's discussion in his two articles on the theme – seems to be common ground among many writers both on educational leadership and on school effectiveness and school improvement. Think again of Fullan on the moral purpose of school leadership

(Chapter 2 above), and of Gold and her colleagues writing of shared values and shared purpose (Chapter 4 above). At least in this sense, it seems to be widely agreed that it is desirable for schools to be communities.

If we think that at least in some sense it is important for schools to be communities built around shared values, there is still the question of what particular values these should be. Strike's discussion of metaphors may seem rather abstract, but he has also sketched (Strike 2000: 637–9; 2003: 84–7) models of three kinds of school, all having a claim to be communities, that may well be recognisable in the real world. The faith school is only one of these, and we have seen above something of what may be shared in a faith school. As regards leadership in such a school, because the school is committed to the beliefs and values of a particular tradition, it would generally be expected that the school leadership above all will be committed to those beliefs and values and will seek to lead the school in the light of them.

It is worth noting that it will make a difference in the real world whether all the members of a faith school do actually share the faith. In Britain that has been a common situation for Jewish schools, Roman Catholic schools and Muslim schools. In the case of Anglican (Church of England) schools, it has often been the case that their intake, as regards religion, has been inclusive rather than exclusive. At the time of writing the British government has made proposals, later withdrawn, that all faith schools within the state system should reserve one quarter of their intake for pupils whose religious allegiance, if any, is different from that of the dominant faith in the school. Such a situation would not necessarily have meant that the declared aims and ethos of a faith school would have had to change, but it would have affected the extent to which the beliefs that underlie those aims and ethos were actually shared across the whole school. The point of the proposal was, of course, to help promote social cohesion by making faith schools more inclusive.

Another of Strike's models is the 'life of the mind' school. Here 'the school community is formed around the realisation of the goods internal to academic practices such as maths, science and the arts' (Strike, 2000: 638). This would be a school that, in the terms introduced in the discussion of educational aims in Chapter 2, is committed to liberal education, where this is understood as an education in the major academic traditions such as mathematics, the sciences and the arts. The shared values of such a community would be the values inherent in these forms of enquiry, engaged in for their own sake rather than for their contribution to external ends. Again, as with the faith school, one would expect the leadership of the school to be imbued with those same values. I think it is possible to imagine a school as a community built around such values, and perhaps there have been such schools, but the model assumes a commitment to the intrinsic value of learning for its own sake, shared by teachers, students and their parents, which is hardly realistic for most schools in modern conditions.

Strike's third model is perhaps the most interesting here, because it puts the weight not on shared religious beliefs or on a shared commitment to learning for its own sake, but on the values of democracy. In this it fits well with the emphasis on another of the aims that we considered in Chapter 2, an aim that many people do now wish to support: the education of active citizens. This school, because it is committed to the values of democracy, seeks to realise those values within the school as well as to prepare its students for participation in democracy in the wider society. It seeks within itself to be a democratic community. Its leaders, therefore, need to be democrats themselves.

If school leaders are democrats in their values, in what way do they lead? Is democracy within a school possible at all?

Here we need to say something about the relationship between community and democracy, and about how far school leadership can be consistent with the values of democracy.

Community and democracy

As the discussion of Strike's models of schools as communities has indicated, a community as such need not be democratic. Here an even clearer case than that of a faith school would be a religious community such as a monastery. Though all within may be conceived as equal in the sight of God, there may at the same time be regulation of the affairs of the community within a structure that is hierarchical – literally so, as it happens, since 'hierarchy' in its origins is rule by priests.

Nevertheless, while a community is not necessarily democratic, there does seem to be some affinity between the ideas of community and democracy. Why should this be so? It is surely because, as we have seen above, a community – unless the term is used in a purely geographical sense – is not just a collection of distinct individuals. A community is constituted by its members who identify with it. It seems natural that they should wish to have some say in the community's affairs. This need not be for reasons of promoting their self-interest as individuals. If they identify with the community, they will wish to see the shared values or goals of the community promoted, so they may very well wish to contribute to discussion about how that is to be done. And to the extent that members are in fact involved in the shared pursuit of the good of the community, their sense of membership of the community is likely to be strengthened.

So, while a community as such is not *necessarily* democratic, the notions of community and democracy can fit well together. We can see this also if we start from the idea of democracy, looking first at the various connotations of that idea. Sometimes democracy is seen simply as one form of political system; generalising a little from this, it may be seen as a set of procedures for decision-making within any institution or organisation. Understood in that way, there is no special connection between democracy and community: the fact that some organisations operate with procedures that give each person a vote on major decisions does not mean that such an organisation constitutes a community in any strong sense. But the idea of democracy can refer to a form of ethos or culture rather than procedures of decision-making. In this sense, if we say that an organisation is democratic we are saying something about the relations between people within it: essentially, that they regard one another as equals in some fundamental way, take each other's opinions and interests into account, are on friendly terms with one another, and so on. An organisation that is democratic in its formal procedures may not be democratic in its culture. An organisation that is democratic in its culture does not have to arrive at its decisions through any particular formal procedures; it may work through informal discussion and consensus rather than voting.

If this makes it seem that there are two quite distinct conceptions of democracy, what connects them is the underlying values on which democracy in either sense can be said to rest. These are values such as the recognition of a fundamental moral equality of persons, and a respect for each individual, so that the basic interests and dignity of individuals are not to be overridden. So, in the formal sense, a system that gives votes to some people but withholds them from others because of their gender or the colour of their skin is not democratic, and in the cultural sense, an organisation in which certain people are looked down on or informally excluded from conversations because of their gender or skin colour – even though they may have the same formal rights – does not have a democratic ethos. At the same time, we can understand a democratic culture to encompass more than this basic respect for individuals as equals. We may think that the culture of an organisation is democratic because there is a sense of mutual belonging, a sense of affiliation between the members and relatively informal and warm personal relationships – and these are just the kinds of values that we also associate with community. It is in this sense, taking the cultural sense of democracy, that democracy and community seem naturally to go together.

This is to see the values underlying democracy in a very positive light. But there are many problems about putting these values into practice in concrete situations. Democracy raises at least the following three issues for school leaders:

1. If the policy that leaders are expected to follow is itself the result of democratic processes, this can make a difference to a leader's thinking about

their responsibility to follow that policy. In Chapter 2 we noted that even the most moral purpose has to be pursued within the context of a broader system, and in Chapter 4 we considered how much space individual leaders may have in which to pursue their own vision for their schools. Should a policy dictated to the school from above – whether at the level of local or national government – always have priority? As we saw in Chapter 4, there can be something attractive in the idea of an educational leader being willing to 'work the system' for the sake of the good of her school and its students, but how fine is the line between this and the leader working in opposition to a government policy that is itself the outcome of a democratic process?

2. If there are certain underlying values that make democracy desirable, the same values do not cease to be relevant just because we are dealing with an organisation smaller than the state. So there are ethical reasons for favouring democracy *within* schools, but there may be reasons on the other side too. We need to consider how far a school can and should be democratic. If it should be democratic in some way, what are the implications for educational leadership?

    As it exists in national politics, democracy is not incompatible with the recognition of individuals as leaders. Most states in the world in the twenty-first century claim to be democracies, and virtually all of them have a president or prime minister who is often referred to as the leader of the country. At the same time, democracy is incompatible with *some* kinds of individual leadership – a leader who cannot be removed from office by popular vote or who governs autocratically is not a democratic leader.

    It is not clear how far the model of president or prime minister will transfer to a school context; we may need a different understanding of leadership in democratic contexts.

3. Schools within democratic societies have to prepare their students for democratic citizenship. That puts responsibilities on educational leadership to pursue the kinds of citizenship aims we considered in Chapter 2, whether or not those responsibilities are explicitly written into government policy in the form, for instance, of prescribed courses in citizenship.

All three of these problematic points are illustrated by the following example, taken from the book on the ethics of school administration (in the American context) by Strike, Haller and Soltis (1998: 91–2).

Case study: A values curriculum

The teachers and principal in a school decide to introduce a course in values education that will help teenage students to cope with issues of alcohol, drug abuse and sexual relationships in their lives. (In the English context this would be recognisable as a programme of PSHE, Personal Social and Health Education.) The decision has been arrived at, as important decisions usually are in this school, through democratic process-es: the issue has been discussed among all the teachers, and a consensus arrived at.

However, when the school starts to introduce this course some parents complain. They say it is teaching relativism about moral judgements, and is anti-God and anti-American. They take their complaints to the school board (roughly equivalent to the governing body in England, though the legal position is not exactly equivalent). The school board listens to the arguments of the parents and of the teachers and decides, by a majority vote, that the school should stop teaching the course.

The teachers are furious. At their next meeting they vote unanimously to carry on with the course in defiance of the school board. And they expect their principal to communicate this decision to the board.

The principal considers himself to be democratic in his leadership style; he would not normally think of going against the unanimous consensus of the teachers. But in this case, the alternative is to oppose a decision that was democratically arrived at within the school board, a body that represents the parents and the local community.

What should the principal do?

This scenario illustrates the three issues mentioned above. First, the school board itself is part of a democratic system, the purpose of which is to see that the interests and opinions of parents and the wider community are represented. However imperfectly that system may work (and it is unlikely that any democratic system is perfect when assessed in terms of the values that make democracy desirable in the first place), it is not clear whether the school can be justified in opposing the school board's decision. (Strike, Haller and Soltis themselves argue that the school would not be justified in opposing that decision; not everyone will come to the same conclusion.)

Second, the case raises problems about how far the staff of the school can constitute a democratic community. The teachers (in the fuller account that Strike and his colleagues give) consider that they have profes-sional educational expertise on their side. They are in fact claiming what we called in Chapter 3 the authority of knowledge and expertise. It seems to make sense that as a professional community they should come to their decision collegially, through discussion. But the professional community of the teachers does not coincide with the whole community of the school (which includes the students as well as non-teaching workers). Why are the arguments for democratic decision-making not extending beyond the teachers to the involvement of all who will be affected by their decisions?

At the same time, the principal's position is not like that of a president or prime minister elected by the people; he was in the first place put in position by the school board, not elected by the teachers, let alone by the whole school community. Elected leaders are meant to be accountable to the people who elected them, but the school principal who respects democracy has to be accountable in two directions: towards the rest of the school, and towards the wider community (we shall say more below about the problems this raises).

Thirdly, the problem in this case arises because both the teacher and the parents recognise a responsibility for the moral development of the young people concerned, but they interpret this responsibility in different ways. The staff want to implement a course that will help the students to engage in critical moral thinking as they face moral issues in their own lives. The parents who protest also want to see their children develop into citizens of good character, but they have a different view of what constitutes good character and good citizenship.

If the dispute could be seen as purely one over how the students should be taught, then the teachers' claim to professional expertise would have a lot of weight. But the dispute is actually more about matters of religion and morality. On this, the teachers do not necessarily have any better claim to authority than the parents.

Democratic leadership

We often think of democracy as being about *who* makes certain decisions (perhaps all of the people affected, or perhaps a majority). But we have also seen that democracy is not incompatible with leadership, and leaders often do have to make decisions. What makes a leader's decision-making powers compatible with democracy is that the leader is accountable to others for the decisions he or she makes.

Democracy and accountability

The case described by Strike and his colleagues has brought out some of the difficulties in accountability. The principal has responsibilities towards the wider community and therefore an accountability *outwards and upwards*. School principals have to show that their school is conforming to laws and regulations and meeting targets that are set by government (local or national). The government in turn is ultimately accountable (within a democratic political system) to the electorate. This does not prevent actual systems of accountability being bureaucratic rather than democratic in spirit. (See Fielding (2001) for a critique of the 'democratic deficit' in the school inspection system in England.)

If we expect democratic government to be accountable to those governed, then we also have to recognise that school leaders are in the position of government in relation to those they are leading. They have an accountability not only *outwards* and *upwards* but also *inwards* and *downwards* towards others in the school. Those others will include not only the staff employed in the school but also the students taught. While there is much talk of accountability to the wider community in contemporary educational management and leadership, we hear relatively little about processes by which school leaders may be accountable to all those over whose employment and education they have responsibilities. But we certainly need to consider this if we are to take seriously the idea of democratic leadership. In other words, we need to consider how far the practices of leadership and management within a school can be exercised democratically.

What we have said so far gives us two important questions about democracy within schools.

- *How can a wider range of people than just the school principal or senior managers have an input into decision-making?*
- *How can those who do make the decisions be accountable to others?*

One possibility is for both of these questions to be addressed through formal structures within the school. A meeting of the staff of the school may be a forum in which decisions are actually made, or it may be a forum in which the principal explains and justifies the decisions that he or she is making (and, of course, it may cover both, since there may be some decisions that are for the principal alone and others that are decided by the whole staff).

The same is true for formal structures that involve the pupils in a school. Many schools in many countries have experience of *school councils*, in which pupils come together to discuss matters of concern to them. Such councils most often are organised as *representative* bodies: a small number of pupils may be elected from each class or from each year. A council of pupils will be able to debate an issue that affects them within the school and will hear what the principal and senior managers have to say about the issue. The pupils may have no powers beyond that, but in some cases pupils have been given decision-making powers over certain – usually relatively minor – matters. In all cases, the extent of the decision-making powers that can be given to pupils, or indeed to staff, will be constrained by the legal responsibilities of the school principal.

So far we have been talking about formal structures by which a degree of democratic decision-making and accountability may be realised within a school. But if we think of democracy in the cultural sense that was mentioned above, then the difference between a democratic school and an undemocratic one will not be a matter of formal structures but of the way in which people relate to each other and take each other's points of view into account informally. Can an informal culture provide enough accountability? That is debatable, because while everyone may be happy with an informally democratic culture for much of the time, the lack of formal structures of accountability means that there is no guarantee that the interests and views of particular people will not be overlooked.

Is democratic leadership just another leadership style?

In Chapter 5 I referred to the well-known idea that there is a variety of leadership styles. The list mentioned there recognised instructional, transformational, moral, participative, managerial and contingent styles.

How does the idea of democratic leadership relate to these styles? Is it different from all of them? Incompatible with some of them?

In Chapter 3 we looked at the idea that there are certain desirable personal qualities in a good leader.

Are there special qualities needed for a democratic leader?

In the rest of this chapter I shall begin to offer some answers to these questions and some further questions that arise from them. I shall borrow some ideas from Woods (2005), whose book should be read for a much fuller view of democratic leadership in education.

Democratic leadership involves a recognition that many people have a contribution to make to policy- and decision-making. Because of this, democratic leadership involves a recognition that leadership can be to some degree 'distributed' among several or many individuals. Does this mean that 'democratic leadership' is equivalent to the term 'distributed leadership', which has become popular in some of the recent literature? Not necessarily, because distributed leadership may come about for various reasons and does not necessarily rest on any particular set of values. As we shall see below, the values that democratic leadership rests on do make a difference.

As a leadership style, democratic leadership may be seen to have connections with the ideas of moral leadership and participative leadership. Such interconnections are not surprising; indeed to some extent, while different terms are used by different writers, they may be different terms for similar ideas. It would be a mistake to try to give rigid definitions of notions such as 'democratic leadership' and 'moral leadership' without expecting overlaps.

A more substantial question arises from Hargreaves' suggestion, considered in Chapter 5, that a school leader should be able to choose the most appropriate leadership style for the circumstances.

Is democratic leadership just another style that leaders can adopt as and when it suits their purposes?

To answer this, we need to look again at the reasons why democratic arrangements may be adopted, remembering that democracy is not just about procedures but also about underlying values. It would be possible for a school principal to set up democratic structures simply as a means to an end – on the basis, perhaps, of research indicating that a democratic school is likely to be an effective school, where effectiveness is measured in terms of results (some evidence of this sort is reviewed by Woods (2005: 27–31)). If the reasons for adopting democratic forms were only instrumental in this way, then changing circumstances, or different evidence about effectiveness, could lead to a change of policy. Such a principal would not be motivated by any deep commitment to democratic values; he or she would indeed be treating democratic leadership as just one style among others. The democracy in this principal's school might be rather artificial or contrived, like the *contrived collegiality* of which Hargreaves (1994) has written.

Instrumental reasons for valuing democracy can be contrasted with *intrinsic* reasons (Woods, 2005: 32–45). We have intrinsic reasons for valuing democracy if we see it as the only way of organising a society or an institution that is compatible with human autonomy, dignity and equality. A leader who sees democracy in this way will be constantly striving for the development of democracy, even though other forms of organisation and decision-making may be easier or more effective towards instrumental goals. Fully worked through, a democratic approach to educational leadership is a radical approach, as Woods makes clear.

Not surprisingly, writers who value democracy for intrinsic reasons tend to see democratic leadership as a form of leadership that is not just one among a number of alternatives, to be weighed in the balance for its advantages and disadvantages, but is *the* form of leadership that can realise all that is best in other forms. This does not mean that democratic leadership offers any simple resolution of problems in other approaches. It may even be the most difficult of all approaches to realise to its full potential. It is not something that can be laid superficially over the existing structure or ethos of a school; it has to go deep, affecting the whole life of the school. Working out its practical implications is bound to be complicated.

Summary

To summarise this chapter, we have looked at the school as potentially a community, seeing a community as being held together by shared values. We have considered what sorts of values these might be. In particular, we have explored how far a school might be a democratic community, and we have recognised some of the issues that this idea raises for leadership within such a school and for the relations between the school and the wider community.

To sum up, the idea of democratic leadership includes a distinctive vision of the kind of place a school can be, and that vision can offer guidance – but never a precise blueprint – on the various questions about values that we have encountered in this chapter.

Suggested further reading

Bottery, M. (2004) *The Challenges of Educational Leadership: Values in a Globalized Age*. London: Paul Chapman. Chapter 9 'Learning communities in a world of control and fragmentation', provides a critical evaluation of the case for seeing schools as communities.

Dewey, J. (1916) *Democracy and Education*. New York: Macmillan. Chapter 7, 'The democratic conception in education', provides an influential view of democracy as 'more than a form of government; ... primarily a mode of associated living', exploring the implications of this for education.

Sergiovanni, T. (1994) *Building Community in Schools*. San Francisco: Jossey-Bass. By one of the leading American proponents of a values approach to educational leadership. See especially Chapter 7, 'The classroom as a democratic community'.

Strike, K. (2003) 'Community, coherence and inclusiveness', in Begley, P. and Johansson, O. (eds), *The Ethical Dimensions of School Leadership*. Dordrecht: Kluwer. The more accessible of the two pieces by Strike referred to in this chapter.

Strike, K., Haller, E. and Soltis, J. (1998) *The Ethics of School Administration*. New York: Teachers College Press. Relevant to all of the issues in this book. The general principles and arguments discussed are just as relevant outside the USA.

Woods, P. (2005) *Democratic Leadership in Education*. London: Paul Chapman. An in-depth and up-to-date discussion of the arguments for democratising schools and the implications for school leadership.

| References

Begley, P. (2003) 'In pursuit of authentic school leadership practices', in Begley, P. and Johansson, O. (eds), *The Ethical Dimensions of School Leadership*. Dordrecht: Kluwer.

Begley, P. and Leonard, P. (eds) (1999) *The Values of Educational Administration*. London: Falmer.

Blackburn, S. (2001) *Being Good: A Short Introduction to Ethics*. Oxford: Oxford University Press; also published under the title *Ethics* in the Oxford University Press *Very Short Introductions* series.

Block, P. (1987) *The Empowered Manager*. San Francisco: Jossey-Bass.

Bottery, M. (1990) *The Morality of the School*. London: Cassell.

Bottery, M. (1992) *The Ethics of Educational Management*. London: Cassell

Bottery, M. (2004) *The Challenges of Educational Leadership: Values in a Globalized Age*. London: Paul Chapman.

Brighouse, H. (2006) *On Education*. Abingdon: Routledge.

Bryk, A. and Schneider, B. (2002) *Trust in Schools*. New York: Russell Sage Foundation.

Busher, H. and Barker, B. (2003a) 'The crux of leadership: shaping school culture by contesting the policy contexts and practices of teaching and learning', *Educational Management and Administration*, 31 (1): 51–65.

Busher, H. and Barker, B. (2003b) 'The nub of leadership: managing the culture and policy contexts of educational organisations' – see http://www.leeds.ac.uk/educol/documents/00001867.htm.

Carter, C. (2002) 'School ethos and the construction of masculine identity: do schools create, condone and sustain aggression?', *Educational Review*, 54 (1): 27–36.

Coleman, M. (2002) 'Managing for equal opportunities', in Bush, T. and Bell, L. (eds), *The Principles and Practice of Educational Management*. London: Paul Chapman.

Coleman, M., Qiang, H. and Yanping, L. (1998) 'Women in educational management in China: experience in Shaanxi Province', *Compare*, 8 (2): 141–54.

Creemers, B. and Reezigt, G. (1999) 'The concept of vision in educational effectiveness theory and research', *Learning Environments Research*, 2: 107–13.

Day, C., Harris, A., Hadfield, M., Tolley, H. and Beresford, J. (2000) *Leading Schools in Times of Change*. Buckingham: Open University Press.

Dewey, J. (1916) *Democracy and Education*. New York: Macmillan.

Fielding, M. (2001) 'OFSTED, inspection and the betrayal of democracy', *Journal of Philosophy of Education*, 35 (4): 695–709.

Foreman, K. (1998) 'Vision and mission', in Middlewood, D. and Lumby, J. (eds), *Strategic Management in Schools and Colleges*. London: Paul Chapman.

Foster, W. (2003) 'Vice and virtue: the value of values in administration', in Samier, E. (ed.), *Ethical Foundations for Educational Administration*. London: RoutledgeFalmer.

Fullan, M. (2003) *The Moral Imperative of School Leadership*. Thousand Oaks, CA: Corwin Press (Sage).

Glover, D. and Coleman, M. (2005) 'School culture, climate and ethos: interchangeable or distinctive concepts?', *Journal of In-service Education*, 31 (2): 251–71.

Glover, D. and Law, S. (2004) 'Creating the right learning environment', *School Effectiveness and School Improvement*, 15 (3–4): 313–36.

Gold, A. (2004) *Values and Leadership*. London: Institute of Education.

Gold, A., Evans, J., Earley, P., Halpin, D. and Collarbone, P. (2003) 'Principles principals? Values-driven leadership: evidence from ten case studies of "outstanding" school leaders', *Educational Management and Administration*, 31 (2): 127–37.

Greenleaf, R. K. (1996) *On Becoming a Servant Leader: The Private Writings of Robert K. Greenleaf*, eds D. M. Frick and L. C. Spears. San Francisco: Jossey-Bass.

Gronn, P. (2003) 'Greatness and service: antimonies of leadership?', in Samier, E. (ed.), *Ethical Foundations for Educational Administration*. London: RoutledgeFalmer.

Habermas, J. (1990) *Moral Consciousness and Communicative Action*. Oxford: Polity.

Harber, C. and Davies, L. (1997) *School Management and Effectiveness in Developing Countries: The Post-Bureaucratic School*. London: Cassell.

Hargreaves, A. (1994) *Changing Teachers, Changing Times: Teachers' Work and Culture in the Postmodern Age*. London: Cassell.

Hargreaves, A. (2003) *Teaching in the Knowledge Society*. Milton Keynes: Open University Press.

Hargreaves, D. (1999) 'Helping practitioners explore their school's culture', in Prosser, J. (ed.), *School Culture*. London: Paul Chapman.

Haydon, G. (2007) *Values in Education*. London: Continuum.

Hill, A. (2005) 'New children's czar vows: I'll stamp out the bullies', *The Observer* (London), 13 November.

Hodgkinson, C. (1978) *Towards a Philosophy of Administration*. Oxford: Blackwell.

Hodgkinson, C. (1991) *Educational Leadership: The Moral Art*. New York: State University of New York.

Jeffery, B. and Woods, P. (1998) *Testing Teachers: The Effect of School Inspections on Primary Teachers*. London: Falmer.

Kouzes, J. and Posner, B. (1996) *The Leadership Challenge*. San Francisco: Jossey-Bass.

Lee, M. (1999) 'Education in Malaysia: towards Vision 2020', *School Effectiveness and School Improvement*, 10 (1): 86–98.

Leithwood, K., Jantzi, D. and Steinbach, R. (1999) *Changing Leadership for Changing Times*. Buckingham: Open University Press.

MacIntyre, A. (1992) *After Virtue*. London: Duckworth.

McLaughlin, T. (1999) 'Beyond the reflective teacher', *Educational Philosophy and Theory*, 31 (1): 9–25.

Mirembe, R. and Davies, L. (2001) 'Is schooling a risk? Gender, power relations, and school culture in Uganda', *Gender and Education*, 13 (4): 401–16.

Nias, J. (1999) 'Primary teaching as a culture of care', in Prosser, J. (ed.), *School Culture*. London: Paul Chapman.

Noddings, N. (1984) *Caring: A Feminine Approach to Ethics and Moral Education*. New York: Teachers College Press.

Noddings, N. (1992) *The Challenge to Care in Schools*. New York: Teachers College Press.

Orchard, J. (2004) 'What Is a "Vision"? Do Good Headteachers Need One?' Unpublished conference paper, Institute of Education, London.

Peters, R. S. (1966) *Ethics and Education*. London: Allen & Unwin.

Peterson, K. and Deal, T. (1998) 'How leaders influence the culture of schools', *Educational Leadership*, 56: 28–30.

Prosser, J. (ed.) (1999) *School Culture*. London: Paul Chapman.

Richmon, M. (2003) 'Persistent difficulties with values in educational adminis- tration: mapping the terrain', in Begley, P. and Johansson, O. (eds), *The Ethical Dimensions of School Leadership*. Dordrecht: Kluwer.

Richmon, M. (2004) 'Values in educational administration: them's fighting words!', *International Journal of Leadership in Education*, 7 (4): 339–56.

Schön, D. (1983) *The Reflective Practitioner*. London: Maurice Temple Smith.

Sergiovanni, T. (1994) *Building Community in Schools*. San Francisco: Jossey-Bass.

Sergiovanni, T. (2005) *Strengthening the Heartbeat: Leading and Learning Together in Schools*. San Francisco: Jossey-Bass.

Smith, M. (2002) 'The School Leadership Initiative: an ethically flawed project?', *Journal of Philosophy of Education*, 36 (1): 21–39.

Stacey, R. (1992) *Managing the Unknowable*. San Francisco: Jossey-Bass.

Starratt, R. (1993) *The Drama of Leadership*. Bristol, PA: Falmer Press.

Stoll, L. (1999) 'School culture: black hole or fertile ground for school improvement?', in Prosser, J. (ed.), *School Culture*. London: Paul Chapman.

Strike, K. (2000) 'Schools as communities: four metaphors, three models, and a dilemma or two', *Journal of Philosophy of Education*, 34 (4): 617–42.

Strike, K. (2003) 'Community, coherence and inclusiveness', in Begley, P. and Johansson, O. (eds), *The Ethical Dimensions of School Leadership*. Dordrecht: Kluwer.

Strike, K., Haller, E. and Soltis, J. (1998) *The Ethics of School Administration*. New York: Teachers College Press.

Talbot, M. and Tate, N. (1997) 'Shared values in a pluralist society?', in Smith, R. and Standish, P. (eds), *Teaching Right and Wrong*. Stoke-on-Trent: Trentham.

Tedesco, J. (1994) 'Knowledge versus values', *Educational Innovation*, 78 (1).

Ungoed-Thomas, J. (1996) 'Vision, values and virtues', in Halstead, J. M. and Taylor, M. J. (eds), *Values in Education and Education in Values*. London: Falmer.

Ward, R. (1990) 'Human greatness', *Journal of Australian Studies*, 27: 1–7.

Weber, M. (1968) *Economy and Society: An Outline of Interpretive Sociology*. New York: Bedminster Press.

Willower, D. (1992) 'Educational administration: intellectual trends', in *Encyclopedia of Educational Research*. Toronto: Macmillan.

Woods, P. (2005) *Democratic Leadership in Education*. London: Paul Chapman.

Wright, D. (2001) 'Leadership, "bastard leadership" and management: confronting twin paradoxes in the Blair education project', *Educational Management and Administration*, 29 (3): 275–90.

Index